secrets
of a

Style
Diva

A Get-Inspired Guide
to Your Creative Side

Published by Cool Springs Press, a Division of Thomas Nelson, Inc.
P.O. Box 141000, Nashville, Tennessee, 37214

Cataloging-in-Publication Data is available.
ISBN: 1591862566

First Printing 2006
Printed in China by Palace Press International

Creative direction by Susie Coelho

Illustrations by Kristi Smith and Aruna Rangarajan;
    Anderson Thomas Design, Nashville, Tennessee — www.andersonthomas.com

Design by Emily Keafer and Kristi Smith;
    Anderson Thomas Design, Nashville, Tennessee — www.andersonthomas.com

Cover Photo by Charles Bush; Los Angeles, California — www.charlesbush.com

Visit the Cool Springs Press website at www.coolspringspress.net
Visit Susie Coelho's website at www.susiecoelho.com

secrets
of a
Style
Diva

A Get-Inspired Guide
to Your Creative Side

SUSIE COELHO

COOL SPRINGS PRESS
A Division of Thomas Nelson Publishers
Since 1798

www.thomasnelson.com

To Hutton and Hailey, the loves of my life.

I love you both so much for being there for me and for allowing me to pursue my dreams and not make me feel guilty when I'm not able to be with you. I hope that in return I can help guide both of you to pursue your passions in life and create your dreams no matter what they may be. I want to help you make those dreams come true, and as a Mom I feel the greatest gift I can give you is encourage you to think outside the box, express yourselves with no restrictions and become the individuals you are. I promise to always provide an environment where you can create freely and make your dreams come true.

I love you!
Mom

Table of Contents

How the Style Diva Got Her Groove On

I'm often asked how I got into this business and how I became a Style Diva. Honestly, it's always been about following my heart and instincts: I just love the world of style, and I love helping and inspiring others. I value every experience life has given me— good and bad. It's been an interesting path, to say the least, and I am thankful that I was able to figure out how to bring together all of my earlier life experiences so that I could live and breathe my passion every day.

Since this is a book of secrets, I will let you in on my first confession. When I first sat down to write this book, I wrote a simple short introduction "From Susie," but soon I realized I wanted to say more and more. When I was done, I had written half the

book, as I kept remembering special moments of my life that I wanted to share! Then, I was ready to tear it up, or at least delete it from my computer. There I sat, by myself at midnight, wondering if anyone would even care. Maybe people would think it was self-serving or egotistical. Or worse, what if they just laughed at my life (and not because of its *I Love Lucy* zany

moments)? Even those of us with the utmost confidence have our moments of self-doubt. Everyone does.

But when my staff and coworkers read through it the next morning, they had a very different take. "Wow, we didn't know any of this," they said. They said my stories inspired them and gave them hope. They could see how each life experience built on previous ones, and that style success does not necessarily happen overnight. I'm always telling them that life is a creative process and that everyone has the ability to create. Now they really saw why I said that all the time!

They reassured me that others would be inspired by this story as well. So I decided that I was willing to share the aspects of my life that led me to where I am today—even ones that are personal, special, and intimate. I hope these words inspire you, get you thinking, and help you adopt a Style Diva attitude so that you find joy in everything you do.

First Tango in Paris

The first lesson I ever received on the ways of a Style Diva came from my mother. She taught me that if you want something badly enough, you'll find a way to make it happen. For instance, when I was about twelve years old, she decided that the family should move to Paris. She found my dad a job at UNESCO, a United Nations organization, and the next thing we knew we moved overseas. When she made up her mind about something there was no stopping her.

To this day, I still love Paris and always long for my next visit. It is one of the most exciting cities in the world and it stimulates my senses in every way! Because I was twelve, I was at the prime age to soak it all in. I loved the little outdoor markets, cafes and parks.

In particular, I adored the park in our neighborhood. It was one of my favorite places to go after school. I would feed the pigeons and just watch people walk by. I'd observe the way they dressed, spoke and acted. I'd play a game with myself: I would see if I

could guess where they were going and what their lives were like. Sometimes it was clear and other times it wasn't. When it wasn't, I'd make up the details of their stories for myself, based on clues I gathered by observing them. To this day when I am traveling and in a new city I look at homes and try to imagine how those people live.

There was always a group of French children who came to the park after school. I watched them more carefully than I watched anyone else. How I longed to make a connection with them! But I didn't speak a word of French. I did eventually discover the universal language of trends, though. Determined to make an impression, I brought over my Troll dolls! These hot American imports were enough to break the ice, and soon I had my first French friends.

I got them hooked on those whimsical, neon-haired little dolls,

and they got me hooked on French style. (I think I got the better end of the bargain!) Within days, I told my mom I just had to have a French bob haircut. The next week I wanted stockings and little heels like one friend; lip gloss and blush like another. My insightful mother recognized that, as a twelve-year-old in a new place, I was a budding Style Diva, eager to incorporate the influences around me into my own life. Rather than refusing to let me experiment, she helped me learn how to pick the styles

mama, I must have those kitten heels!

S'il vous plaît
S'il vous plaît
s'il vous plaît

that worked for me and showed me how to work them into my life—without losing the sense of who I was and where I came from.

Those years in Paris were some of the best and most influential years of my early life. It's no secret that Paris is the epicenter of style and fashion, but in my time there I became more than just a spectator. I learned to enjoy the simple things that life has to offer and to live my life fully and stylishly every day—the way the French do.

Manic Mannequins

We returned to Washington, DC, from France after three years. I was heartbroken to leave Paris so my mom wanted to find something that would keep me connected to the world of fashion and style. She took me to join the Teen Board at a department store. At that time, this was an innovative program that let selected teens play

with and show off the current fashion styles. It may have been a far cry from the runways of Paris but it sure beat pretending to be on the catwalk in my room! I jumped at the chance to try on and work with all these clothes.

On Saturday mornings, my mom would drop me off, and the other board members and I were told that we could pick out anything we wanted to wear. We would go around the store and pull together wild combinations—just to experiment. Then we would accessorize with belts, scarves, jewelry and shoes. We'd fan out through the store, striking and holding poses like mannequins. (People would even poke us to see if we were real!) When we got bored with an outfit, we'd change and start the entire process over again.

It was an energizing and inspiring experience because we were free to create what we wanted. No one told us that anything we did was wrong. We each put together outfits based on our own unique sense of style. As we encouraged each other, there was a freedom of expression—the more outrageous the outfits the better. This provided a great foundation and a certainty about the next stage of my life: I was going to be a model.

College Un-bound

When I was eighteen years old and going to American University, my mom encouraged me to enter a beauty pageant. "Mom, I am so not the beauty pageant type," I informed her. "Blonds with big breasts and shapely calves win pageants." "Well, you never know," she said. Turned out I was right about the blonds, but I did win Miss Photogenic over the other fifty contestants. There was hope for me yet.

The photographer took some shots of me and brought them to the prestigious Ford Modeling Agency in New York City. The next thing I knew I had dropped out of college and was off to New York by myself. To this day, I thank both my parents for believing in me, giving me my independence, and trusting that I would make it. Although I expected to get modeling work right away, reality soon set in: work was slow to come. Not being one to just sit around, I got a job answering Alice Cooper's fan mail to make extra money. I dragged the huge mailbag from the post office, down Fourteenth Street to my apartment on Fifth Avenue. I was a bag-lady stylin'.

It was a tough time for me, but I kept my chin up. I missed my family and my mother's dinners. There were nights I was so lonely that I would cry myself to sleep. But then the next day would come and I'd put on my smile and head out again. I was determined to make it. I wasn't going to quit!

One day in Bloomingdale's,

I ran into a famous model I'd seen in magazines for years. I'll never forget her—or her clothes. She wore a striking monochromatic outfit, beautifully layered, with various textures. Everything was tone-on-tone cream, so sophisticated and elegant. Even her handbag matched. She had on these expensive suede boots—at least they looked expensive—and I could envision her toting shopping bags full of incredible things back to her fabulous uptown apartment and getting ready to go out on the town with friends at some chic new restaurant.

The model didn't even notice me as she made her way to the escalator, confident, elegant, and self-assured. In that outfit, I would have been confident too! The lesson hiding in my Bloomingdale's Moment became apparent. I decided right then that when I got my first check I was going to go out and get myself back in the style groove I'd been in all my life. I had always loved creating my look and my life, and now I had stopped. What was I waiting for—something or someone else to change my life? I needed to take charge again and create!

New Coast, New Horizons

Next stop was Los Angeles. Isn't that what all models want to do—become actresses? I signed up with another modeling agency right away and started working while I took acting classes. The change of venue was good for me. Modeling jobs were flowing in; I was even traveling back and forth to New York for work.

One Memorial Day weekend, my roommate and I decided to take off for Palm Springs for a getaway. That weekend I met my first husband, Sonny

Bono—an event that changed my life. I was taken by his tenacity, his sense of humor and—believe it or not—his sense of style. He had fantastic taste in just about everything, including homes. His house in Palm Springs was filled with Indian fabrics and organic textures. Just the kinds of things I grew up with. That house was small and quaint and I felt right at home.

Our Bel Air home was another story. It was a grand Italian villa. I'll never forget the first day I drove up to the house. Everything was on a huge scale—big gates, long driveway, high ceilings, and enormous rooms. It was almost empty except for the bedroom and breakfast room. It was a huge decorating challenge!

Luckily we had a famous decorator on board. I was excited, but also a little overwhelmed. There was so much I needed to learn, but our decorator was a good teacher. When he finally did the installation, he sent us out of town. When we came back four days later the entire house was done all the way down to the smallest detail—furniture, rugs, drapes, plants, decorative accessories, paintings, everything. It was a makeover of all makeovers (I can relate to the joy that homeowners feel when my television team and I swoop in to remake their backyard in one day.) I'll never forget the impact that it had on my life and the incredible feeling of seeing it empty one day and then completely pulled together with music playing and candles glowing!

While I loved our homes, I also spent lots of time with realtors looking at other properties just to see what was out there and to get inspired. So, while other people went to the beach on the weekend, we would go house shopping, even when we had no immediate intention of moving. We looked at one-hundred-year-old farmhouses, fixer-uppers in the mountains, stone cottages among the redwoods and desert hideaways. We always looked for inspiration, and these browsing expeditions fueled both of our imaginations.

Some people can live happily ever after with their house being "done." Not us! We were ready for a new challenge. We sold the Bel Air home to purchase the rustic four-acre property just up from the Beverly Hills Hotel. The plan was to build a new home from

scratch. The property also needed a ton of landscaping. While I had owned a greenhouse at the Bel Air home and had grown orchids, I was a bit of a novice with larger plant material. Of course, that didn't stop me! I figured I would learn as I went. You thought perhaps the "Surprise Gardener" had a formal degree in landscaping? Nope, I learned the hard way—by doing my own backyard! I know firsthand what it's like to be looking at a barren plot of land and hoping that the plants you've picked out will work. That's one of the reasons why later I loved helping other homeowners on my gardening show.

Guess Who's Coming for Dinner?

I was shooting a TV movie in Hawaii when I got a call.

"Guess what? We're in the restaurant business."

Sonny had always dreamed of opening a little mom-and-pop Italian restaurant where he could serve his famous Steak Bono, a classic family recipe. Dreams often come and go

with most people but not with him. Although I was working as an actress at the time, I didn't love the amount of down time that is inherent with an acting career. I was bored. I hated waiting around for auditions or the next scene. I wanted to *work more*, not just sit around waiting for something to happen.

Well, now I had some real—and hard—work to do. There was a restaurant to build, style, and run. I was on my way to my next adventure.

We had to choose a direction for the style of the restaurant before we could even begin construction—floor tiles couldn't be chosen, paint couldn't

be bought, nothing could happen. We knew we wanted a relaxed, fun, and inviting atmosphere. I thought back to my modeling experience in Milan and recalled the wonderful little trattorias where I ate. Inspired by my memories, I chose a Mediterranean palette featuring a burnt orange, dusty sage and cream combination. (To this day I still love these colors.)

Next up were such details as dinnerware, glassware, flatware, tablecloths, and napkins. The choices for linens in particular nagged at me; the color selection was so poor. The typical red, dark green and white. Those didn't work for me. I asked the vendor to dye tablecloths in our signature burnt orange color. (This was the beginning of my wanting to design my own products!) One decision led to another. For the wait staff, I designed long aprons in the same burnt orange. I also used bromeliads as our flowers to give the room an exotic feel, but I put them in small, low vases to keep the style casual. And I kept going, returning to my image of the Milan trattorias for inspiration

whenever I got stuck.

You have to understand that neither Sonny nor I had a clue about the restaurant business. Yet we dove in headfirst, talked to those who had more experience, used the information we gathered, and trusted our instincts.

Wolfgang Puck was already having great success with Italian nouvelle cuisine in his famous Spago Restaurant, which was just up the street. He was an innovator in this genre and supported our mission. Sometimes I would head over to Spago for a bite and to chat with him about food and the biz—the restaurant biz, that is. He always had encouraging words of wisdom. In the end, we had a hugely successful Italian trattoria with a waiting list every night.

Lights, Camera, Change

While we had the restaurant, I landed my first job as a television host. It was even more fun than acting. The show was a biography/variety program for which I interviewed people like Julio Iglesias and Mikhail Baryshnikov. The format of the show called for me to interview the celebrities in their homes. They'd then perform at the show's studio, and the broadcast would combine the two segments. (Getting to travel, see fabulous homes and meet legends—can you say *dream job?*) Each star had very different tastes, and sometimes the personalities of their homes were surprisingly different from their on-screen persona. Sometimes this was an interesting revelation about each star's personality; other times it was just... well... surprising. It was sometimes shocking to me that people whose careers were built around their personas could have homes that were so different than expected. A space that didn't reflect its occupant never felt much like to a real home to me, no matter how expensive or finely decorated it was.

Meanwhile, the show was a success, and my career continued to expand. At the same time, though, my personal life took a turn. Sonny had been a huge inspiration to me, and I remember very fondly my nine years with him. But the time had come for me to find myself and create my own life outside of his world.

A Star Is Worn

I set out on my own path and opened a clothing store a few blocks away from the restaurant. But not just any clothing store. My place, A Star Is Worn, took all those once-worn outfits that fill celebrity closets and put them to good use. Having been photographed a lot at events, I knew firsthand that you can't be photographed in the same outfit more than once. You will certainly get dissed by an editor. Through a program I termed Clothes Aid, I took the celebrity problem of too many clothes and helped solve other, more pressing ones in the world. Profits from each sale went to the donating celebrity's favorite charity.

It was a good business idea that was also a good idea for helping others. But that creative idea had to be reflected in the décor of the store. Since it was all about stars and Hollywood, and television and movies, I decided to design it like the back lot of a movie studio. The floor was done like the Hollywood Walk of Fame with stars and names stenciled on the concrete. In the back was an old west façade with a saloon door as the men's changing room and a bordello on the other side for the women's.

Even before I found the store location, I was recruiting clothing from those I knew in Hollywood. John Travolta, being a true gentleman, had his driver drop off the white suit he wore in all the publicity photos for *Saturday Night Fever*, and he even included a framed, signed copy of the *Time* magazine cover to authenticate the suit. Cher, Farrah Fawcett, Rene Russo, and Angelica Huston all gave me clothing and it grew from there. You need supporters in any new venture and they were my first supporters. They had to trust that I would represent them and these items in a proper way to the press as well as to the public. I am forever grateful to them for believing in me and the concept of the store.

But a little success doesn't mean that you don't have to stay on your toes. One day while I was working on finances and had my head buried in paperwork in the store, the phone rang. The sales girls were busy, so I picked up the phone, and a somewhat gruff voice blurted out, "This is Lucille Ball." "Yeaaah, right." I replied. The voice on the other end replied, "I have a gown that I want to donate. It's black and beaded, and I wore it to the last Academy Awards." Oh my gosh, it *was* her! My idol! I had seen every episode of *I Love Lucy*, and here she was on the phone, not an assistant or secretary but the *real Lucy!* I tried to recover quickly. "I'm so sorry...I'd...we'd... be very happy to pick it up Ms. Ball. Can I get your address?" I knew her address already because I drove past her home every day on the way to mine. But mortified by my goof, I kept that little secret to myself. I ended up sending my manager to pick up the dress as I was embarrassed by the way I had acted on the phone. My experience in retail taught me how to think creatively on my feet—and a bit about customer service as well!

Not So at Home on the Range

I eventually remarried and had a son. Motherhood triggered my next decision (or rather, the insomnia induced by mothering a colicky baby while nursing every two hours around the clock, and after having been on bed rest for five months). I decided we were moving to a ranch forty-five minutes outside of town. It was quiet and peaceful and I was hoping to finally get some sleep. Plus my husband loved to ride horses.

Perfect...or so I thought!

On the ranch, we had horses and chickens. Being a city girl, I'd never tended livestock, but I was game. (I'm always game!) After a few weeks I realized my chickens weren't laying eggs so I took off for the feed store to find a solution. I told the guys behind the counter that my rooster had an underactive libido. They just laughed. "You sure you got a rooster," they asked? I wasn't sure. Could it be the white one with the hairy legs? They fell to the floor laughing.

"Come on, guys," I said. "I have chickens and I want eggs." Finally they told me, "Lady, a hen don't need no rooster to lay eggs—only if you want fertile eggs." I felt so stupid. Did I miss that in school? So they gave me a better feed mix and sent me on my way.

The next step was learning how to tend to the horses and pick their hoofs—not the most pleasant task, considering what they walk around in. Let me tell you, the fun really starts when the horse decides he wants to be frisky and kick.

I was used to the big city—Paris, DC, New York, Los Angeles—and here I was cleaning horse hooves and trying to figure out where the rooster came into the egg-laying process. What was wrong with this picture? (Hmmm, an awful lot.) I turned to what I knew. I decided to remodel the house, raise the ceiling, and landscape my two acres. I did that, and quickly lapsed back into boredom. What had happened to my life? I thought I would like this life. I mean, who wouldn't? I didn't have to work, and I had lots of time on my hands. Oooohhhh. That was the problem!

I loved working and I hated having extra time. I loved creating and action. The busier the better, with me. This was just not my style! I realized that it was okay that I had explored this path, as I learned even more about who I was. The experiences on the ranch confirmed how I wanted to live. Which was not this way. So that was it. We were moving!

Time to Get Back to Work

I was ready to get back to work. But I'd been out of the business—every business—for over four years. I pondered how I would start again. What should I do? I'd been a model, actress, television host, restaurateur, storeowner, and now rancher. Was there a connection with all of this? I sought help by calling my friends. I wanted their opinion on what they saw and what they thought I could and should be doing.

"Style" kept coming up as the predominant word. "You motivate, you help, you're stylish, you have a wealth of experience, and you inspire us." Wow! I'd never thought of that as a profession. I decided to do what I loved, what I'd been doing all my life—work in the world of Style.

I told my agent that I was a style expert and was finished with interviewing other celebrities. I wanted to host a style show and if it meant starting at the bottom again, I would. Within a few weeks of making that decision, I landed a television show on Home and Garden Television (HGTV) called *Surprise Gardener*. It was a one-day garden makeover show and one of the first in the genre. Then my show *Outer Spaces* followed. I was on HGTV for ten years.

Don't ever let anyone tell you that it's too late to follow your dreams.

Now on my third book, with four others in the works, I am finally sitting down to write what people have been asking me to write for years. I'm ready to pass along my knowledge, secrets, and advice. To all of you Style Divas out there: be passionate, create, and push your boundaries every day so that you can maximize your potential and have a fuller and more stylish life.

E-mail me through my website and stay in touch. By the time you finish this book I suspect you will know me well—better than most—and I will also want to know you. We are now friends and need to support each other. I am here to guide and help you fulfill your dreams and be your styling buddy!

Meet Your Style Diva

What Is a Style Diva? When I refer to a Style Diva, I'm not talking about some rich celebrity or someone who has tons of money, wears designer clothes, and only buys high-end items. Or somebody who doesn't lift a finger except to dial the most expensive decorator in the city. That's not a Style Diva; that's a style snob—and she's on the opposite end of the spectrum.

No, the Style Diva I'm talking about is not necessarily rich. She may not know the latest trends or be super-knowledgeable about style. She just has to have the energy and a passion to express herself and create a more stylish life. Everyone has the potential to be a Style Diva!

As you can see, I never planned on being a Style Diva. I didn't get a fancy degree in style, or study it at a top university. It just happens to be that, in any big endeavor I've undertaken, I have never worried about how I was going to do it. That was the easy part, learning along the way. Deciding I was going to do it was the hardest part. Knowing how to do it was secondary. Over the years, I have established a way of living my life and a creative process that brings passion, excitement, joy, energy, and love to everything I do. I'm lucky enough to be able to live my life to the fullest—and so can you. How?

The first step in becoming a Style Diva is to decide that you already are one. It's as simple as that. Decide to embrace your own unique sense of style. Decide to embrace life with passion and newness. Decide to adopt a stylish attitude. By attitude, I don't mean, "I'm so cool and you're not." I mean to look at everything you try with a positive, enthusiastic, can-do spirit. I mean be willing to express yourself and say who you really are. A Style Diva never apologizes for her creative process. She knows she doesn't have to be perfect. She knows she doesn't have to match every color correctly or arrange furniture in just the right way. A Style Diva's not afraid to make mistakes.

Declare your divadom as your birthright. Then you can do the things you need

to do to reach your full style potential. Once you live your life from a Style Diva's perspective, everything is infinitely more exciting.

For example, you can walk into the restaurant you always go to but see it and experience it in a whole new way. You can decide, "I'm going to really explore this menu, notice the décor, experience new foods. I'm going to get to know the waiter and find out all about the specials, the wine list and even the desserts! I'm going to try something new and get the most out of the experience and come away with a new appreciation of dining out." Now you can add all this input to your style repertoire and draw on it when you need to.

A Style Diva makes the decision: "I may not have a lot of money or time, but I'm still going to have a great home." She will search high and low for a way to get the task done. She doesn't worry about not looking cool,

doing things herself, or buying someone else's discarded items. She sticks to the course and is proud when she accomplishes something. Her point of view is strong and she doesn't take no for an answer.

A Style Diva uses the five Senses of Style that you will learn in this book, and this grounds her styling and gives her confidence. She might try one approach, scrap it in the middle, and try another. She might call in a team of experts to help her with some details. She might get everything done and, at the last minute, decide she needs to make some significant changes. There will be barriers, creative blocks, critics and naysayers, and yet a Style Diva will always stay the course, loving the journey.

On Style Myths, Lies, and Procrastination

Do you find you have excellent excuses as to why you could never be a Style Diva? After all, (you wonder) what do you know about style? You may feel like you were born without the "style gene" that others have. I've seen it time and again—struggling Style Diva hopefuls who sabotage their dreams with myths, lies, and procrastination.

I've isolated five of the most common stalling tactics. These are the myths you may believe about style and about yourself that need to be confronted and conquered!

Classic Stall Tactic #1
I've got a creative block.

The term "creative block" shouldn't even enter a Style Diva's vocabulary. You are always creating—whether that's figuring out what shoes to wear or making your kid's lunch. The reason that you say you have a block is two-fold. First, sometimes you're just plain spent—you're exhausted and hungry. Take a nap or get a snack. Second, you need a change of scenery. I find that the best way to de-block is to pick up a magazine or book, go to a museum or gallery, take the dog out for a walk, or just get in my car and drive.

Classic Stall Tactic #2

I can't afford to be stylish.

You can't afford not to. Invest in yourself. Being stylish does not have to be an expensive endeavor, especially in this day and age of flea markets, garage sales, and discount stores. I shop at them all the time. In fact, most Style Divas I know are always looking for a good deal—and, believe me, they know where to find them. You don't need money to be stylish, you need ingenuity. Part of the joy of being a Style Diva is figuring how to get the most bang for your buck. A Style Diva might go to a thrift store and find a funky old vase for five dollars, take it home, mix it with a few other objects, and make a huge statement. Where others might see junk, she sees a masterpiece.

Classic Stall Tactic #3
I'm waiting for inspiration to hit me.

I hope you brought a change of clothes because it's going to be a long wait! You can't sit around hoping that inspiration will strike. You need to go out and find it. It's in the magazines and books you read, the movies you see, the clothes you wear, the places you travel, the friends you admire, the dreams you have. It's all around you 365 days a year, 24/7. Trust me, there is no shortage of inspiration; there's just sometimes an unwillingness to embrace it.

Classic Stall Tactic #4
I just don't have the time.

The pursuit of style does not have to be a time-consuming endeavor. You can spend ten minutes a day on it and still feel like you've accomplished something. The important thing is to block off a certain time once a day, once a week, even once a month, when you can devote your attention entirely to style. Turn off the cell phone, turn off the computer, turn off your Blackberry, turn off the television, and turn on your Styling Self. This could be anything from jotting down all your ideas that day in your Style Journal to tacking up photos on your Style Board. I'll explain more about those later.

Classic Stall Tactic #5
But I'm not an artist...I can't even draw a stick figure!

Neither can I! In fact, my daughter draws circles around me. I always thought I wasn't an artist because I couldn't draw. I now know that's not true. You don't have to be Picasso to have style; you just have to be willing to understand the elements that make up something artistic and stylish and be willing to learn by doing. A Style Diva is always creating something from nothing—whether it's a floral arrangement as a centerpiece, or a home. A Style Diva embraces art in every sense of the word and thus is an artist!

Style Divas Unite!

Although my Style Diva adventures haven't always been easy, I've persisted by believing in myself, building doors where there were barriers, and remaining tenacious about my vision. (Oh yeah—and I had fun whenever I could!) And you know what? It paid off. I love being a Style Diva, and I wake up every morning happy to start creating. I am thrilled to be finally passing along to you my innermost secrets and hope that these will help you fulfill your creative dreams.

style diva quiz

We all have a Style Diva living within us—but some of us are more in touch with her than others. This book will enable you to start tapping into that relationship. The Style Secrets will get your head into the Diva Zone and by doing the Diva Drills you will start to live your life the way an artist does—creatively. I also have online Diva Tools to help you build on what you learn in this book.

Where are you on the Style Diva Scale? The first thing you need to do in order to learn how you can bring your most stylish self into the spotlight is go to **www.susiecoelho.com** and take the Style Diva Quiz (shown below). Your points will be calculated automatically and your profile will appear. You'll also find Diva Direction to help you best use this book to flex your style muscles and build your confidence. Take the quiz online. One of the profiles is you!

Preview the quiz:

Answer each of the following questions as honestly as possible—there are no right answers, just choose the ones that best reflect how you approach style.

1. **When you're at the park or out for a sunset walk through your neighborhood you:**

   a. *Notice the silhouette of branches against the sky.*

   b. *Run through the huge list of to-do's in your mind, while alternately checking your Blackberry and pedometer to make sure you don't miss a message or a step.*

   c. *Take it all in—the kids playing, the couples canoodling, the new plantings—then realize you've gone the wrong way!*

2. **For your next dinner party, you want to have a strong floral centerpiece. You visit the local florist and:**

   a. *Ask them to do something similar to the one they did for your last party—it was a big hit.*

   b. *Ask them to make something up for you; their judgment is probably better than yours.*

   c. *Ask them to copy the one you saw in your favorite magazine.*

3. The best way to describe the dishes you use for entertaining is:

a. A huge, varied collection. Your reasoning: "I'm always picking up something new, and then, you see, I have to find other stuff that matches, and..."

b. A cohesive set of dishes of a specific style that works with both your home décor and the type of parties you usually host.

c. Disposable.

4. You put together monochromatic outfits by:

a. Mixing a variety of fabrics, textures, and tones—a boucle jacket with a sleek pair of pants, perhaps, or a fitted T-shirt with a rustic peasant skirt.

b. Simply pulling a suit out of your closet. You found the designer and cut that works for you, and you wear them nearly every day.

c. Wearing clothes that are the same color, of course.

5. While out shopping at the mall, you wander into a housewares store. You're struck by a specific display of dinnerware, glassware, utensils and linens that are set out as if the party were about to begin. You:

a. Wish someone would invite you to a party like that.

b. Contemplate buying the entire ensemble and ask the sales person to please give you a table plan so you can set it just as they have at the store. It's exquisite!

c. Admire it for a while, perhaps buy one element that works with what you have, or just move on.

6. How comfortable do you feel turning to someone for style advice?

a. Very—I try to get as many ideas as I can!

b. I'm selective about whom I ask; I have one or two people whose opinions I've come to trust.

c. Not at all—I'd be embarrassed to have people find out how uninformed I am.

7. There's a room or space at your home that's just not done. You're holding off because:

a. It's easiest to just close the door or avoid spending time there.

b. I have about a dozen ideas for what to do with it, I just haven't settled on one yet.

c. I'm waiting till I can do the whole thing over exactly as I envision it.

8. How often do you feel you have to be *right*?

a. More often than I actually am.

b. Not that often—I'm pretty open to hearing others out and seeing things from their perspectives.

c. Well, I usually am.

9. The best way to describe your attitude toward shopping for yourself is:

a. It's fun to go look, but I may or may not buy much, unless I find pieces that really fit with what I've already got.

b. I love going and seeing everything, but I either come home with too much or nothing at all.

c. It's like taking a final exam; I know there's a right answer out there—I just don't know what it is!

10. It's Saturday afternoon, and the kids announce that they are "BORED." You:

a. Pop in a video for them and get back to your work.

b. Take them for a walk, play a board game, or color with them. You have a standard repertoire of boredom beaters.

c. Crack open the multiple kids-crafts books you own and let them pick several that appeal to them.

11. Perfection is:

a. Something I actively strive for.

b. Impossible.

c. Something others can achieve, but not me.

12. How regularly do you clean out closets, clear off your desk, review stuff you've saved?

a. I totally ignore it unless the piles get the better of me.

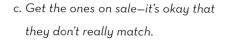

b. *About twice a year, which reminds me how much I love my stuff!*

c. *I organize it in ways that are aesthetically pleasing, which means clutter never really gets the better of me.*

13. It's the start of the season, and the catalogs have arrived in bulk in your mailbox. You:

a. *Go through every single one of them, dog-earing everything you like.*

b. *Put the whole pile into the recycle bin immediately.*

c. *Pull out the one or two that you regularly order from and the one your best friend has recommended, then throw the rest away without looking at them.*

14. You're buying new containers for your patio garden. You:

a. *Get the ones that match the style you already have.*

b. *Get the ones that look most like the ones in the latest garden magazines.*

c. *Get the ones on sale—it's okay that they don't really match.*

15. How often do you change around your living room?

a. *Once a year, when we put up the Christmas tree.*

b. *When I can't escape the fact that the current layout doesn't work, as everyone keeps banging their shins on the coffee table.*

c. *I haven't moved the furniture in a while, but I usually swap out vases and accessories seasonally.*

16. You have piles of seashells the kids have collected over the summer. At the end of the season, you:

a. *Throw them away when the kids aren't looking—like you need more junk in the house!*

b. *Create some sort of display with the best of them, then toss the rest.*

c. *Put them in a shoebox, promising yourself you're going to find something to do with them.*

17. You're watching a televised broadcast of this year's big home design show. "Orange," they tell you, "is the *hot* color for the year." Your reaction is:

a. *"Orange?* **Orange?** *I don't own any orange. Time to go shopping!"*

b. *"Orange?* **Orange?** *Why* **orange?** *Who comes up with this stuff, anyway?"*

c. *"Orange.* **Orange.** *Hmm. That's an interesting color. Maybe—well, no. It just won't work with everything else. Guess I'll just have to wait till next year to be in."*

18. When friends or family give you a gift for the home, how well does it usually sync with your other belongings?

a. *Almost perfectly every time. My nearest and dearest know what I like in my home. And when it doesn't—well, that's what eBay's for.*

b. *Since all the other stuff I put on display has come from them, they sync pretty well!*

c. *I've never really focused on things matching—I'm more the eclectic type.*

19. If someone were to say to you, upon visiting your home, that they never would have thought you'd own a particular item, your reaction would be to:

a. *Explain it was given to you by someone else.*

b. *Tell them it's part of a hot new design trend.*

c. *Smile and make a note to yourself to dispose of the item immediately because it doesn't work.*

20. This weekend's to-do list includes finally framing and hanging some of your family pictures. The part of the process that hangs you up is:

a. *Reworking other items in the room to balance the new additions.*

b. *Deciding on the right arrangement.*

c. *Finding the right frames.*

21. **When shopping, how often do you pick up various items that interest you?**

a. Sometimes, although I usually ask the sales people to show things to me.

b. Often—I need to get a feel for what I'm buying and to lay things out as I'd actually use them.

c. Mom always said, "Look with your eyes, not with your hands..."

22. **You've finally settled on a paint color for the living room. Your sister tells you she's not a big fan of it. Your reaction:**

a. Your husband picked it out, and if she has an issue with it, she can go talk to him.

b. She doesn't have to live with it, so who cares?

c. Take her to the paint store and have her help you pick something else out.

23. **You'd consider redoing a room because:**

a. Redoing? I haven't gotten it done in the first place.

b. The walls are marked up or the furniture is getting worn.

c. You have some out-of-town friends coming for a visit and you want it to look its best.

24. **Okay, that project didn't turn out at all like you had hoped. You:**

a. Throw it away, paint over it, do whatever it takes so no one sees the disaster.

b. Live with it.

c. Start over, following a plan that's more like what you've successfully done before.

25. **You use pillows and throws on sofas, love seats or chairs to:**

a. Keep warm and comfortable when sitting on them.

b. Reinforce and finish the room's look.

c. Bring some of the latest trends into your home.

Reminder: Take the quiz! Go online to www.susiecoelho.com and get your personal Style Diva profile.

Get Inspired

When I tour the country on speaking engagements, I'm often asked, "Susie, can you please come to my house? I need help!" I would love to visit everyone's home, but it's just not possible—unless I put on a red and white suit and get some reindeer. Instead, I'll let you in on where my inspiration comes from and give you a sneak peek at how, for example, I come up with new ideas that I use in all areas of my business.

What's my secret? There is actually no secret to it at all. Inspiration is not hidden; it's all around us in books, magazines, catalogs, movies, markets, and nature. It could even be on a tube of toothpaste. You just have to look for it.

People often think way too much before they embark on a style endeavor. They wait for inspiration to hit them, like a magical, creative sledgehammer. A Style Diva doesn't wait around for inspiration to find her. She actively goes out and grabs it.

This section of the book is designed to help you find the path to your own inspiration. Along the way, you'll learn how to come up with innovative ideas and clear your mind of the barriers that block your creativity. There are many different roads to style and many different creative processes, but one universal truth stands: it all begins with inspiration. Let's go find some!

the first rule of style

One common concern shared by many Style Diva hopefuls is that they don't know the rules of style. You think there's got to be a rule book, right? Don't we have guidelines and boundaries? You may be thinking that being a style expert is all about creating rules for the rest of the world to follow. I'm here to tell you it doesn't work that way.

The first rule of style? *There are no rules!* In order to truly stimulate your style senses and have unlimited creativity, you need to be completely free of restrictions. So let go of those preconceptions.

Rules may be necessary in the exterior world—in our government and laws—but in the realm of ideas and imagination, they're null and void. **Rules create boundaries and promote rigid thinking. They stop the creative process dead in its tracks.** In any artistic endeavor—be it painting or singing or styling—as soon as you try to put rules on creativity, it comes out stale and lifeless.

When I was growing up, I remember people telling me, "Red and pink clash—never put them together." What about Valentine's Day? Pinks and reds

Diva DRILL : Rule It Out

What are the rules that Ms. No-Way has dictated to you about style? What style rules do you simply take for granted? Make a list of the do's and don'ts that you've been adhering to up until now. Here's a warm-up:

- You must use white tablecloths for formal occasions. (Only if you're 90!)
- Don't wear white after Labor Day. (What about Winter White?)
- You must buy matching pieces of furniture for a room. (Nope.)

dominate this holiday and generally are mixed. What about a beautiful garden full of English roses in pinks and reds? Do you walk by and say, "Those pink and red rose bushes were planted together? They clash!" Of course not. My six-year-old daughter has dresses and jackets with this combination. A Style Diva beyond her years, she would let me know if this mix was off. So much for that rule!

There's a voice that many promising Style Divas fall prey to—I'll call her "Ms. No-Way"—who dictates what "must" be done, or throws up barriers to exploring and expressing style. She's the voice that tells you,

"You can't mix those two china patterns," or "White carpets aren't for houses with children," or "To have a room, you must have walls." Many well-meaning individuals in your life may have trained Ms. No-Way, but that doesn't mean she is Ms. Know-It-All. **Without evaluating the truth for yourself, you might be stuck with these rigid notions that stop you from creating to your full potential.**

• Fabric, curtains, or pillows are only for interiors. (What about outdoor rooms?)

Now take your list and circle the rules that you've never been happy following. These are the rules that you've felt constrained by or that have slowed down your creative impulses. That negative reaction is your Style Diva striving to speak. Listen to her!

Just say "No!" to Ms. No-Way!!

see the chance, take it

Far too often, our minds are so focused on the future and on busy work that we allow inspirational moments—or life in general—to just pass by. **Sure, Style Divas look ahead and stay focused on projects, but they also know how to live in the moment.** They realize the value of stopping to try on fabulous Manolos, whether or not they plan to buy them. They understand the importance of not rushing a conversation with someone truly interesting, of watching their kids splash in a rain puddle, or of accepting a taste of a new cheese at the gourmet store. It only takes a few minutes, and the payoffs can be enormous. **Being receptive to those small moments opens us up to new inspirations, information, and opportunities.**

My associate, Ryan, always reminds me of the time we were in New York City on a business trip. After dinner that evening (at 11:30 pm!), I insisted that she go with me to the top of the Mandarin Oriental Hotel. Why? Because from the lobby on the thirty-fifth floor, you get the most spectacular view of Central Park and I felt she *had* to see it. Although she was exhausted, she allowed me to drag her up there.

Exiting the elevator, Ryan saw Central Park as she had never seen it before. She felt a surge of exhilaration, and she was no longer tired. She went on and on about the view, thrilled with the city and the lights. The side trip had been worth it. She now shares this experience with her friends and has dragged many a weary one to the top of that hotel. **The secret she learned? Never pass up a moment that can become a wonderful memory!**

"You have to see it! It's the most fabulous view of Central Park!"

Diva
DRILL : Just Say Yes

Say yes to an experience to which you might normally have said no. Next time your girlfriends want to go dancing, pretend you're not too tired and just go and enjoy the experience. Are the kids begging to go to the park, but you know you have to prep dinner? Stop and give yourself fifteen minutes with them. Keep doing this, and you'll find that there's a wealth of experiences and inspirations you might have missed—ones that you wouldn't want to live without.

observe, observe, observe

I get extremely inspired when I travel, and I think this is one of the reasons many other people love travel. By seeing new countries and how others live, eat, and dress, you gain a wealth of inspiration that can influence your sense of style in all areas of your life.

When I was designing my first home collection, the buyers took me to the Maison et Objet in Paris, where designers come from all over the world to see what the trends are for the upcoming year. Ten of us took the train from the city, as the show was just outside of Paris. We later perused the main department stores, such as Les Galeries Lafayette, Printemps, and Le Bon Marché, to see the latest and greatest in home decorating. **This was my idea of a business trip!**

Many stores grouped their brands together by lifestyle. If your style was casual, you shopped on the third floor; if your style was more traditional, you went to the fifth floor, and on it went. (Why can't all life choices be made simpler this way!) I purchased many items

as inspirational pieces simply because I liked the way something was embroidered or because it had a certain color or texture I wanted to remember. London was the next stop for a repeat performance. We shopped on Kings Road in all the big stores—Harrods, Marks and Spencer, Selfridges, and Harvey Nichols.

After London, I headed to Tuscany in Italy, where my brother was on a sabbatical with his family in an old villa north of Florence. What a treasure trove of inspiration! I took pictures everywhere I went, focusing on the ornate doors, rustic arbors, chipped old paint with layers of various colors, sunbleached walls, cobbled streets, plants, flowers, vineyards—anything that would stimulate my style sensibility.

Granted, I've been lucky enough to go to some special places, but once you open yourself up to noticing the world around you and becoming totally present, you will find ideas anywhere and everywhere. **Keep your inspiration radar on at all times, and you will discover new ideas like never before.**

Style Divas see the world as one big window shopping opportunity.

Diva DRILL: Watch and Learn

We're often so involved in our lives that we don't step back and really look at what's around us. A Style Diva, of course, always has her inspiration radar on! Here's a fun way to exercise your observation skills:

Head out to the store at which you most often shop, and pretend you're a detective or a reporter trying to get a story. Before you go in, stop to study the outside of the store, as if you're there for the first time. Stand outside the doors for a short while, watching those who enter and exit. Study what they're wearing, what kind of bags they're carrying, their hairstyles, and their shoes. What do those people tell you about the store before you've even entered?

Next, head to a specific section of the store—for instance, the bedding department. What do you have to walk past to get there? Make a mental note of as many details as you can. Once you're in the bedding department, what's the first thing you see? Study the displays and the way the store has merchandised its goods. Are there new colors? Interesting textures? Notice the types of bedding. Are there appliqués, embroidery, sequins, a mix of textures? Is it a modern look or country or traditional? Perhaps you see one you love; perhaps there's another that makes you think, "I would never have that on my bed!" Note your reactions to everything you see—this is a great way to tap into your likes and dislikes.

Once you've completed your tour of the department, start focusing on specific items. For example, observe the shapes of decorative pillows. What shape are they? Which do you like? Move onto the decorative accessories and do the same.

When you get home, write down everything you remember about the place—make a long list of what you saw as each thing comes to mind. You'll be amazed at how much you were able to take in and how much you learned about yourself!

get smart about art

On one of my *Outer Spaces* episodes, we featured a backyard that looked much like a barren lot. The lady of the house was an artist who loved collecting "stuff." **But she also loved the work of the artist René Magritte, who inspired her with his surrealist style.** Her dream was to create a magical and unique garden reminiscent of his work, so we took on the challenge.

Magritte is famous for his dreamlike portrayals of dapper gentlemen dressed in formal attire, so we carved out a piece of wood that looked like the silhouette of a man in a top hat. This was placed at the entry to her garden and became the gateway to the yard. Next, we created a water feature with a black umbrella, which was both whimsical and dramatic. With the help of a small recirculating pump, the water ran along the top of the umbrella, as if it were rain from the sky, dripping down the edges into

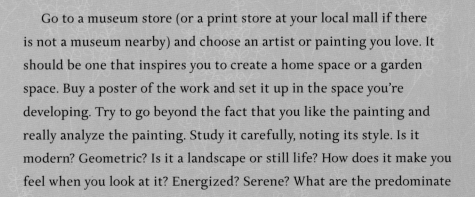

Diva
D R I L L : Start with Art

Go to a museum store (or a print store at your local mall if there is not a museum nearby) and choose an artist or painting you love. It should be one that inspires you to create a home space or a garden space. Buy a poster of the work and set it up in the space you're developing. Try to go beyond the fact that you like the painting and really analyze the painting. Study it carefully, noting its style. Is it modern? Geometric? Is it a landscape or still life? How does it make you feel when you look at it? Energized? Serene? What are the predominate

a small pond that we built.

Our homeowner had a collection of beautiful glazed plant pots, but they were all stacked haphazardly and full of dirt and debris. She had many things, in fact, that she had left piled up for when she had use for them.

We dug through her miscellaneous objects and cleaned them up. We then chose the most interesting shapes and colors and grouped them together on the shelves according to their color, as if they were pieces of art. **We created order out of disarray by identifying a style theme (the art of Magritte) and utilizing available objects to reflect that style.**

Art and artists can be a great source for inspiration. If you are not accustomed to going to galleries or museums, why not start now? Your Style Sense will be stimulated in a new way. And I'm sure many new ideas will find their way to your garden or living room!

colors? Is it bright or dusky in tone? What details in the composition really stand out to you? If it's in a nearby museum, go and spend some time looking at the real thing; that way you'll also be able to better appreciate the textures the artist used. Ask yourself which of these elements are the ones that you find the most striking. Now, you can begin building your ideas for your space based around these inspirations!

keep a style file

As you well know, **creativity can be a random, disorganized, and messy process.** It's important to capture your ideas before they disappear into thin air. A valuable tool for idea management is the personal style filing system. A "Style File" is an orderly collection of images, swatches, fabric samples, and other visual inspirations. Keeping a Style File helps you make order out of chaos and allows you to have a collection of readily accessible ideas. It also helps you put your personal stamp on all your styling projects.

Diva DRILL : File Facts

1. Find a place to put your Style Files—this can be anything from a file cabinet to a leather file box, or even a cardboard banker's box. I suggest something stylish, as it is a Style File, not a dumping bin. It helps if it's easily transportable. You'll want to take it up to the bedroom, family room, or even outdoors. I keep one in my bathroom (bath time is the only time I'm guaranteed peace and quiet).

2. Start ripping and tearing. This is the fun part! Take a few minutes out of your day to snip and tear photos from magazines, catalogs, books, or any other source you can get your hands on. (European magazines are one of my secret weapons.) Remember, you're looking for pages where you love the color, the shape, or the look of something that inspires you. Don't think about it too much—just rip!

3. Organize your inspirations. Put them into different color-coded

Make note of why the items in your file inspired you. Is one a possible piece of fabric for your sofa? A picture of a great kitchen you love? An idea for new bedroom furniture? **Once you have all your inspirational references filed away in an orderly fashion, you will have more confidence about your own style sensibility.**

For my own Style File, I started with folders and now have file cabinets, shelving units, and stacks of catalogs and magazines that I use as my expanded style references. You need these ideas and inspirations at your finger tips, so that you're not searching for bits and pieces that you "remember seeing somewhere." It's really quite simple and it will save you from many a creative meltdown later on.

folders marked: *Outdoor, Indoor, Holidays,* and *Style Don'ts*. The Indoor folder should include ideas for living rooms, family rooms, kitchens, bathrooms, and other rooms. The Outdoor folder should include ideas for entrances, entertaining areas, and gardens.

If you are working on a special project like creating an outdoor living area, then divide the folders according to furniture ideas, flooring ideas, water features, plant material, etc. The *Holidays* folder contains ideas for *Christmas, Chanukah, Kwanzaa, Valentine's Day,* or any other holiday you like to celebrate. The *Style Don'ts* folder is a collection of examples and photos that turn you off. By also including items that you *don't* like, you can prevent expensive mistakes.

Once you have amassed a healthy collection of folders—and for some categories you may have more than one—you can keep them organized in a Style File box or file cabinet. This will be a lot easier than looking for them in clothes pockets, the trash can, or under your sofa!

let mother nature take the lead

If you think about it, Mother Nature is the ultimate Style Diva. Just look at her garden. The color palettes she's come up with for fruits and vegetables are extraordinary. I've used the rich tones of a mango (red and yellow) on many of my more exotic makeovers. The lime green and black seeds in a kiwi represent the perfect contemporary mix. Bell peppers have such bright, vibrant colors—green, yellow, orange, and red! Eggplant inspired my Aubergine ("eggplant" in French) collection of bedding. Spices like cayenne (red), saffron (orange/red), cinnamon (brown), turmeric (yellow), and clove (black/brown) inspired my Spice Market collection. **Most of my bedding collections use botanicals, which are Mother Nature's greatest hits.**

Having spent eight years shooting outdoor shows, I guess I can't help but think of plant material and flowers all the time. They're what I worked with every day, and I am inspired by the color of leaves, the beauty of a rose, or the shape of a seedpod.

Some of my favorite inspirations from the outdoors came from the colors of moss and algae I discovered in a pond. They were the most beautiful shades of lime green I'd ever seen. Lying quietly atop the algae were some small, pod-covered branches. I envisioned this image on a bedding collection, a dinnerware pattern, or even framed as a work of art in my living room.

There are incredible textures in nature, as well. When you look at the texture of a leaf, notice that one side is shiny and the other is usually matte or fuzzy. You can also find a variation of color on a variegated leaf. Thanks to Mother Nature, I'll use a shiny, silky fabric next to a corduroy fabric, or I'll complement a leather jacket with a lace blouse. It's a great way to create layers of interest. **If Mother Nature can mix textures, why can't you?**

Style Divas don't say "purple" or "eggplant"—they say "aubergine"!

Diva
DRILL : Seeing Green

Walk around your neighborhood or a local park at dusk—when the light best captures color. As you stroll (remember, this is an exercise in observation, not perspiration!), focus on the part of the outdoors most of us typically take for granted: the green plant material. Observe carefully the leaves of trees, shrubs, and bushes; cacti and succulents (if you have them); low-lying ground covers, grasses, and ferns; even mosses and lichens on rocks.

Now ask yourself: What do I see? Okay, yes, you see green. But what *kind* of green? Is it greenish-blue? Dark green? Silvery green? Consider the layers, textures, and different patterns of green. Are they smooth, shiny, variegated? How does one green look when overlapping another? Really *see* all the infinite ways green is used in nature. This is the way a Style Diva observes the world.

write away

Because the best ideas can come out of the blue anywhere and anytime, you need to prepare yourself to capture them in your Style Journal. You can't assume you're going to remember an inspiration five hours or even five minutes after it's struck. For this reason, I suggest you create a Style Journal to turn your moments of brilliance into something tangible that you can refer to at a later date. Once you have an inspiration, it's important to take this step. **An idea has more substance when you plant it in the material world.**

Some of my favorite quiet moments are in the bath. This is a great place for me to relax without a cell phone or e-mail. A moment to think! **I keep my Style Journal handy to travel between my bed and bath.** I find that some of my best ideas come when I'm relaxed (or even tired!), so I make sure I'm ready at all times. I never want to let an idea slip away.

Your journal can also include names of stores you want to investigate, sketches, samples of colors or fabric that you think might give you ideas in the future, or anything else that jumpstarts your imagination.

It's time to start a Style Journal! I can hear your practical side telling you that any old notebook will do, but it won't. Just like your Style File, the Style Journal should be an inspiration in itself. Go to a good stationery store, art shop, or bookseller and browse through its selection of journals. Find one that appeals to you with the cover, the feel of the pages, even its smell. It might have lined pages or blank ones, be spiral- or perfect-bound, or be clad in a rich leather cover. This journal should beg you to put your thoughts into it. Be sure that its size and shape make it easy to carry around in your everyday handbag, briefcase, or tote. You should have your journal with you at all times. No excuses!

While you're at it, you might want to buy a pen or marker that is dedicated to your Style Journal. You should always be able to get your thoughts down as they hit, without being distracted by searching for a writing implement at the bottom of your bag. If the store does gift wrapping, have them wrap it up for you, then take it home and open it, just like a gift to your Style Diva self.

other people's style

One of the best sources of style inspiration is other people. I am always happy to share my ideas and resources with my friends, and they do the same for me. We inspire each other. When I was a young model, I worked with a lot of great models, among them, Rene Russo. While she was already a supermodel and had graced many *Vogue* covers before I had even started, we ended up working together and became great friends.

Back in the early 1980s, Rene had a very Bohemian sensibility. Her home décor was eclectic and relaxed, and her personal wardrobe was very much the same. (Truth be told, she is so naturally beautiful that she could wear a rag and look good!) Although we were both living in Los Angeles, we happened to be working in New York at the same time.

One day, we decided to go downtown to SoHo and check out some vintage stores. I found some wonderful items that she convinced me to get, including a few skirts, washed out shirts, and some lace accents.

Rene loved wearing her outfits with flat sandals (as she was already pretty tall); I preferred them with boots or shoes with a little heel. She wore soft,

Diva DRILL: Get a Shopping Mentor

Pick your most stylish friend or acquaintance and ask her to go shopping one afternoon. She'll be glad you did. Stylish people love to shop, and they appreciate it when others ask their advice! While you're out, study how she looks at things when shopping. Observe her process of investigating the options—what makes her decide to head into a certain store or aisle, how she assesses what's around her, what makes her select a given item to try on or examine. Listen to her comments as she evaluates what's around her. Ask her how she made her decision or

flowing blouses; I wore long T-shirts and big belts. **The way we chose to wear them was a direct reflection of our own unique sense of style and our own personal twist.**

Some of you might admire a friend's style but don't want to copy it. After all, you don't want to be accused of identity theft! Don't worry, you can make any style your own. **Some of the best ideas are actually twists on someone else's ingenuity.** And anyway, they say there are no original ideas, so who exactly are you copying? Once you take possession of an idea, you inevitably put your own twist on it, and that is what makes it new and yours!

The same principal holds true in home décor. You can get your inspiration from a magazine spread and try to imitate it, but it will never be exactly the same, unless you have the same house and the same furniture and accessories (a highly unlikely scenario). By the time you're finished with the project, it will be uniquely yours. **So don't worry about "borrowing" other people's ideas to inspire you—they'll be flattered, and you'll be on your way to something great.**

what she finds interesting about it. If you see something you like, ask her opinion on it or ask her to help you match something to it. And listen to the questions *she* asks *you* during that process. Does she ask you in what situations you'd wear something you've chosen, or where you'd put an object? Does she like the color, but a different shape might work better? Pay attention to her approach. You don't have to buy anything, but you'll take home a lot of valuable information.

you shop, girl!

Okay, I know I'm not going to have to twist your arm on this one. **Whenever you feel stuck and creatively blocked, go shopping!** Here's a secret: you don't even have to buy a single item—although I know that might be tough! Usually when most people shop, they go with the clear intention of finding something specific. Their focus is so narrow that they don't see half the

experience *everything* in the store. You could also think of it as free professional advice! Take advantage of this. You may want to go when you have some extra time to roam freely through the aisles, stopping frequently.

When I shop for inspiration, I like to experience all the different colors, textures, shapes, styles, and new trends. I pay attention to the direction of style this season and compare it to last season.

store. This particular shopping assignment I'm talking about is different—it's an *inspiration mission*. You're there to look, observe, and take it all in. Rather than selectively deciding what you want to see and buy—you're there to

What's the hot color that is in every store? What's the popular style that is emerging? Can this style be added to my home? *Let the store inspire you.* **Once you learn to shop this way, each store visit will be full of discovery.**

56

Style Divas See shopping as an adventure.

Even if you were looking at the last store you visited with fresh eyes, you probably still felt comfortable there; it was familiar. You likely noticed things you never saw before, but were you surprised by any of it? Probably not. Now it's time to experiment with the *unfamiliar.* Head out to a shopping destination you rarely, if ever, frequent, such as a village filled with delightful, upscale boutiques, the most chic avenue in your city, or a specialty store known for its fabulous style and perhaps more expensive than one you would normally visit. (Consider not even bringing your credit card—you want to focus on browsing, not buying.)

Stop at each store or display and take a good look at what's there, using the observation skills you awoke in the previous drill. What are the other customers like? What are *they* looking at? Are there floral displays in the store? Have they put out tableware in some whimsical display that you'd never have thought of? Pick up any and every item that strikes your interest, and observe it from all angles. Note its color and shape and how it feels in your hand. Go ahead and talk to the sales associates or store owners if they come up to you. (They won't bite.) Ask them where items have come from and about the artists or craftspeople they feature. At the end of the day, you'll likely be brimming with new ideas and new ways of looking at even the most common items.

57

feeling is believing

We're a very visually-oriented culture, and this means we often rely on our eyes for ideas and inspiration. A Style Diva knows better. When she's in creating mode, she has all her senses working overtime. Touch is particularly important, and it's vastly underrated.

Next time you're out shopping or taking a walk, rather than admire an object from afar, pick it up and get a little touchy-feely with it. **This tactile experience really helps you understand, know, and feel the object in a fresh new way.** It's another form of communication.

For example, say a ceramic bowl catches your eye at the store. You pick it up, and, all of a sudden, you realize this bowl wasn't what you thought it was at all. You're *bowled* over by how light or heavy it is. You also start to appreciate the shape and the texture of the clay. Suddenly, you have a whole new perspective on the bowl than if you had simply looked at it.

The way something feels is very important for influencing Style Sense. Is it rough or smooth? Does it feel

Diva DRILL : Touch Table

Lay out a place setting for yourself using a mix of items you don't commonly put together: a placement from one set; a napkin from another; a bowl or plate from your everyday set; a teacup and saucer from your good china; several different glasses; flatware from several sets.

Now, sit down and put a blindfold over your eyes. Handle each piece as if you were really using it. Notice each one's weight, how it sits in your hand, or how it feels as you lift it to your mouth. Does each piece please you individually? Or are there ones that, now that you can't see them, don't really do it for you? Are there items that felt "matched" with one another, based on their weight, texture, or shape?

warm or cold? Just recently, I went shopping to look at tabletop displays because I needed inspiration for my new collection. I wanted to make sure my product was unique, functional, and stylish. I must have touched every plate I could get my hands on in each store. I would pick it up and notice the weight and feel. Then I asked myself, "Is this the kind of plate that I would like to eat from?" and "Do I like this cup's particular shape? Is the rim thin and more appropriate for a tea party? This plate is heavy. Would it be perfect for a Mexican fiesta?" **I didn't just see the new tabletop design—I could feel it, too.**

Think about what kind of party or mood each piece feels right for. For instance, when you lift a glass to your lips or raise a cup, do you feel romantic and delicate? Or does the item bring to mind a hearty, jovial, or boisterous gathering? Does a time of day come to mind?

See what surprising matches you come up with based on tactile compatibility, and note what events or occasions might be right for these pieces.

put yourself in their pumps

Sometimes when you look at your own home repeatedly, trying to think about what you need to change, it's very hard to make decisions. **Here's how to free yourself: Instead of looking at it from your point of view, put yourself in someone else's shoes and see what she sees—then decide if you like the style message you're sending.**

I tested the accuracy of my own style message when I launched into the lifestyle arena. I called all my friends and asked them what they thought I did for a living. This way, I could see how they interpret my skills and the message I communicate in my business and life.

Have you ever told someone something, and, when they repeated it, the message was not at all what you thought you had communicated? When I write a letter, I don't just think about what I want to say, I also try to

put myself in the shoes of the recipient. I try to choose the proper words for the context and make sure my ideas are clear. If I'm giving a talk, I will often think through the logical questions that I might have about a product and try to make sure something in my presentation answers those questions for my audience.

Using someone else's perspective to get a baseline on your personal style message is an important concept, as all too often we only look at things from our own vantage point. **Sometimes reversing this can give us a much truer picture of ourselves. Don't worry—you might like what you see!**

Style Divas don't apologize ∗∗∗ for their taste.

Diva D R I L L : Decode Your Abode

Take pictures of several of the rooms of your house and bring the prints to your office, a school or community meeting, or some other gathering of people who have not seen your home very often, or at all. Ask them to evaluate the pictures and to give their answers to the questions below. (You can tell them you're hiring a new interior decorator and want input on what others think of her style, which is the truth!)

- Who lives here?
- What style do you see? Would you call it contemporary? Simple? Traditional? Something else?
- Would you say that the style reflects who I am? If so, why? If not, why not?
- What does each room tell you about the person's lifestyle?
- Do you think the rooms work together? Do they seem cohesive, as if they all belong in the same house or with the same person/family?
- If you had to put colors to my personality, what would they be?

You might hear some surprising things about how well (or not) your space matches your public persona. This is not to say that you should change one or the other to fit the perceptions of those around you, but it will give you some interesting insight on the impressions both you and your home are making on others. If there's a big disconnect that you're not pleased with ("You're so creative, but these rooms look really bland!"), that's a clue of where to begin re-styling.

style comes from within

We've talked a lot so far about how to look outside yourself for inspiration. However, many of your most brilliant ideas lie deep within you. You just might not have unearthed them yet. **Style comes from who you are and where you came from, as well as outside sources.** Everybody has a memory bank of ideas and experiences that we accumulate over years of living. These make up the cornerstones of your Style Sense. Obviously, there's a relationship between inner and outer observations. Seeing something new triggers an old memory. The old memory gives you a way to interpret a new trend for yourself and, well, there you go!

A Style Diva is able to tap into her memory bank for ideas at will. As I look around my living room right now, I realize how much of my background has inspired my style. My drapes, for example, are orange, long, and flowing silk. People always comment on how much they love the texture and the feel. These drapes were inspired by my mother's saris. She was from India and used to wear this traditional

Indian dress, with magnificent colors like fuchsia combined with turquoise borders, bright orange, mango yellows, and stunning reds and gold. I always admired their beauty—the colors, the way they hung, and the draping pleats in the front. Years later, when I styled my home, the memory of those saris influenced my entire living space from my drapes to the color of my pillows.

So how do you take out an inspiration loan from your own memory bank? You have to acknowledge your experiences and not be ashamed or afraid to pull from your past. Listen to the voice in your head that says, "That reminds me of the time..." and go with it. This is your trigger, a creative bridge to the past. The Style Diva always listens to those cues.

I remembered all the afternoons I spent as a child ironing my mother's saris, and I had an idea for drapes that sprang from that memory. Your memories can have a powerful influence in the same way. You may have lived most of your life in a simple farming town, but that doesn't make your memories any less vivid or beautiful than mine. Look at the wealth of style that surrounds you—the stacks of hay, the beautiful wheat, the various colors of the horses and cows.

I have a friend who grew up on a ranch out west. Her entire home is inspired by her past because she loves to be surrounded by the rustic nature around her. She has browns and earth tones on her bed, and reds and checkerboard patterns in her kitchen. It's her style statement of who she is and what she is about. That is the main point. **You have style within you. You just need to connect with it.**

Diva DRILL: Picture This!

Go through your albums or scrapbooks and draw out the old photos that feature a favorite scene, room, or piece of furniture. Or pick out shots that have you in a long-forgotten, but then beloved, childhood outfit, or perhaps one that shows your mother or aunt in something that made you think she was the most glamorous person in the whole world. Remember what it felt like to really love the rug or sofa in the photo. Then push yourself to remember what it was exactly that you loved about it. Maybe it was a set of cherries that dangled from the bodice of your fourth grade school-picture dress. Or the way your aunt's coat felt against your cheek when you'd run up to hug her. You may remember the set of glass grapes your grandmother kept on the dining room table—the ones you always wanted to play with.

In these details, you can find a motif, a texture, even a color palette that you can introduce into your rooms now. Once you've identified some meaningful images, keep your photos at hand as constant inspiration. Put them out in a basket or tray on the coffee table, for instance, and add to the pile as you take or find new ones that hold an inspiring image. This way, you can just pull them out randomly to look at them, which will also help you to begin to pull out the meaningful details of the image beyond the linear life story. You could also do this with postcards, greeting cards, and thank-you notes. Periodically revisit your collection and let these memories provide inspirational images for you.

let it flow, let yourself go

The best ideas often come in waves. Once you open the door, there are hundreds of ideas just waiting to come crashing in. In order to be truly creative, you can't put a limit on the number of ideas you have. **You have to be able to hop on your style surfboard and ride.** It doesn't matter if you think some of your ideas are terrible or unoriginal, or you know they aren't going to work. The key is never to put a limit on yourself.

The first idea could be the best, but often it's the most conventional. Let's say you have a bunch of unused terra cotta flowerpots. Ask yourself, "What different uses for them can I come up with?" The conventional answer would be to plant flowers or herbs. **But then think about other options to expand beyond the conventional use.** You can also paint, stencil, or wrap them with fabric to change the color or texture. Group some together on an entertaining table upside down as a stand for a platter. Use them to hold potpourri or coins. Paint them in seasonal colors and add grasses and eggs for Easter or bulbs for Christmas.

Diva DRILL : Brainstorming Session

You don't want to leave ideas swirling around in your brain forever. That will just jam your circuits (and you know how lousy that feels). So clear up your mental jams by routinely getting your ideas down on paper. Here's how to start. Get a kitchen timer and head to a space in your home that you feel needs a lot of work. Set the timer for fifteen minutes. Now, with your Style Journal in hand, settle down and just

Or use them in a sandbox as a shape for sand castles. In the office, the pots could hold various sized paper clips, stickies, or pens. Or they can serve as a doorstop. Attach them to a wall by the drainage hole in the bottom and use them to hang belts and such. (Indulge me. We can always throw some ideas out later!)

This is true brainstorming, and one idea can lead to another. Sometimes the last idea is the one you'll like the best. Sometimes you might go back to the first or the fourth. **It doesn't matter which one you ultimately choose—the important thing is that you're creating and using your imagination. That's the creative process that I love!**

begin to list all the things you could do with that room. Paint it, move furniture, get rid of the pile of junk in the corner, whatever. At the end of the fifteen minutes, review the list for a single task or item you want to work with. Set the timer for fifteen minutes again, and begin riffing on all the different ways you can imagine doing that task, or myriad uses for a particular object, as I showed you earlier with the terra cotta pot example.

never say no

In the world of ideas and inspirations, the word "no" is a destructive force. In fact, a Style Diva knows to *just say no to no* (say that fast, five times). Don't give in to the easy trap of negativity. **The worst thing a creative person can do is edit herself before she has even started.** In the brainstorming phase, you must hang on to every idea like it's a precious stone. It may not mean anything to you now, but you never know how it might come back and delight you later.

Diva DRILL : Dream the Impossible Dream

Go to your list of ideas from the "Brainstorming Session" Diva Drill. Choose the one that your practical, rational (and maybe a bit negative?) self tells you is the most far-fetched, impractical, you-could-never-make-it-happen idea. For instance: You may want to build an outdoor kitchen. But you have no idea how to get started, nor do you have the budget. And there's that voice inside you (remember Ms. No-Way?) saying "This is way out of your league!"

First, indulge in a little visualization exercise. Find a peaceful place and close your eyes. Imagine your inner Style Diva sitting across the table from Ms. No-Way. Let Ms. No-Way have her say, bringing up the barriers or fears you have about the project.

For instance, your dialogue might go like this:

MS. NO-WAY: It's never going to work.

STYLE DIVA: We'll never know until we try it.

MS. NO-WAY: You don't even know where to begin.

STYLE DIVA: I'll do some research.

MS. NO-WAY: And then what? You'll never afford it.

STYLE DIVA: We'll break the project into stages, and do what we can in steps.

MS. NO-WAY: It'll never get finished.

STYLE DIVA: Well, if we don't start, it sure won't get finished. Want to see the floorplan?

Suddenly, you're seeing blue skies and chicken on the grill, and it's time to take the first steps toward that outdoor kitchen.

Let your inner Style Diva speak louder and louder, until you feel confident that you can hear her over Ms. No-Way. This is your dream and she's not going to keep you from it! While you may not be able to execute your dream right now for any number of valid reasons—time, money, other resources—that doesn't make the idea worthless. Our dreams are what drive us, and by allowing yourself to think of the project in stages, you may find the insights you need to finally realize your dream.

try clutter therapy

Clutter is a Style Diva's enemy. Why? Number **one:** it feels uncomfortable to be in a space that's cluttered. Number **two:** it takes up all your attention. Number **three:** you spend all this time searching for a brush when you should be painting.

In order to be free creatively, your head and your home have to be clear of distractions. If you walk into a room where you want to be creative and the first thing you see is stacks of magazines, bills, or assorted projects that you swore you'd finish last week but didn't, how can you be focused?

But what if you walk into a room and the magazines are stacked neatly, bills are paid, and that project you wanted to complete last week is actually finished? Imagine how that would

feel. Suddenly you can focus all your attention on figuring out the color scheme for
that wall, rearranging the furniture, or just
writing a list of all the creative ideas you had

that day. **Get rid of clutter, and you gain
the freedom to accomplish your goals.**

Diva D R I L L : Love 'Em or Leave 'Em?

Choose a room to work on, one where you've got a lot of stuff. Sort every object in it. (Bigger items can be "sorted" in your journal for now.) Tackle everything from large items like carpets and couches to small items like vases and picture frames and sort them into the following categories:

1) Love It/Can't Live without It/Want to Be with It Forever

2) Kinda Like It/Admire It/Feel It's a "Nice Piece"

3) Never Liked It/Seemed Like a Good Thing at the Time but the Romance Is Over/Want to Break Up with It Immediately.

Now, for every item you placed in the first category, get specific about why you love it.

Do you love the color? The texture? The shape? The style? Asking yourself these questions helps you figure out not just what you love about a certain object but also your preferences as a whole. Does a certain color predominate on the list of beloved items? Does a specific texture pop out as a recurring theme?

Do you love it because it has loving connotations? In other words, did someone you love give it to you? In this case, ask yourself whether you really love the object, or if it's the person connected with it. If it's the latter, is this something that truly makes you happy, or is your real love affair with the person connected with it? (If you love the object and the person, that's fine—but if not, move it out of this category!)

For every item in the second category, pinpoint what you do and don't love about it:

• Is it there because you merely felt it was "nice" and the "right thing to have"?

• Is it there because you paid a lot for it and don't want to admit you wasted your money?

• Does it have some of the same attributes as the item you love, but there's one

thing you can't stand about it (for instance: love the color, hate the shape)?

- Was it great once but is now worn out, broken, faded, or in need of repair?

If any of the first three reasons apply, get ready to say goodbye. Remember: We're going for "love" and "like very much" here, folks. So don't let unsuitable suitors (even if everyone else says they're great) hang around and sap your energy. For the fourth reason, ask yourself whether the item can be salvaged and whether doing this would change your feelings about it. If not, then it's time to part with it.

For every item in the third category, figure out why you're still holding onto something you dislike or even hate:

- Did it come from someone you love and you don't want to hurt his or her feelings? Did your partner bring it into the relationship and you want to keep the partner, not the stuff?
- Does it have sentimental value?
- Has it just been there so long that it's just become part of the scenery?

Now, review why you're keeping these items in the third category and compare them to some of the items you've discovered you don't love as much as you thought. Are they all from one particular person? Is there another way you can bring that person into the room? If you're keeping items from your beloved grandmother that don't match your style, perhaps you could write about the heirlooms in your journal and give them to another relative, or instead, hang pictures of your grandmother that include those same items.

Now that you have your lists in your journal, identify which items from the second and third categories you can get rid of immediately. Box up small objects that have no place in your life anymore (hello, eBay!). Hand your partner his collection of softball trophies and tell him to display them in his office, and give grandma's antique cordial glasses to your niece who is outfitting her first apartment. Clearing just a few of the things you dislike from the room can give you a whole new perspective on it.

71

don't ignore your instincts!

Now that I've shared some secrets about how to develop and organize your inspirations, you should be well on your way to Style Divahood. But there is one insight I want to pass on that is essential to building your success and confidence: Don't ignore your instincts. There will be many barriers and hurdles, but as a Style Diva, you can't allow them to throw you off course. Trust your instincts and never ignore your gut feelings. Over the years, I've learned to trust my instincts in everything that I do. **Even though at times they may seem to defy reason, my instincts and my intuition have always been my roadmap.** One of the most vivid examples of this is the inspiration that was key to adopting my daughter Hailey. After I had my son Hutton (and after five months of bed rest), we decided to adopt our next child. We wanted a girl. I knew that in order to keep myself going until we were connected with her, I would have to visualize how she would look

and act. I wanted to get a sense of her to make her more real for myself. In my mind, I imagined her with brown, wavy hair and a fair complexion.

One day, I was shopping in Palm Desert and I passed a children's clothing store. A dress caught my eye, and I just stood in the middle of the sidewalk staring at it. Although I didn't have a daughter yet and it made no sense to buy a child's dress, my instincts told me to go into the store and purchase it—so I did. It was the most beautiful little white sleeveless cotton summer dress I'd ever seen. Attached was a sash with little flowers. The same flowers laced the bottom of the dress.

That little dress was bought on a whim but became my most significant purchase in a long time. I took it home and hung it in a place where I could see it every day. **I opened my closet door in the morning and there it was. It reminded me of the little girl I dreamed about, and each day she became more and more real to me.** I could picture her in the dress, running around in my bathroom and bedroom. The

72

more I saw the dress, the more I thought of what life would be like with her in our home. Shortly thereafter, the phone rang. It was a call from the adoption service—they had found a baby girl for us. Three months later she was born.

I now understand the importance of bringing home that little dress. It enabled me to visualize my dream more vividly. **I've also learned to trust the little voice telling me to do something that may seem completely irrational but also seem completely right.** These are very special moments and ones to treasure. They can help move you forward in life toward achieving your goals and objectives, whether those are life-changing decisions or just casual changes in your living room. Hailey wore that dress until it was so small and tight that she couldn't get it on. The dress was a miracle, and so was Hailey.

Diva DRILL: Trust Your Gut

Go out shopping. No list, no needs, no have-to-haves—just go out. Unlike some of your previous shopping exercises, though, your mission is to buy something. As you go through the stores, using the new observation and investigation skills you've been building, let yourself be open to the items around you. When you see something that grabs you, grab it. Maybe it's a candle or a serving dish or a flowerpot. Buy it anyway. This is your instinct speaking to you.

At home, set the object in front of you and open your Style Journal. Write down what that object represents to you. It may not be clear at first glance, but eventually it will **become** clear. The candle stands for a romantic evening you long to have; the serving dish reflects a really festive, happy, family gathering; the flowerpot represents the patio and garden you'd like to have. Write out the whole story, envisioning the story turning out with a positive ending. Pay attention to how the object you purchased plays into your story and, especially, how it can help you achieve your dream. When you've finished, put your purchase somewhere highly visible, where you'll see it frequently throughout the day. Let it remind you of what you're dreaming of and how you see it coming out.

believe in yourself

There are many people who ac-complish great things without knowing how to do them before they start. They don't let the fact that they might not know how to do something stop them. One of the best examples of this I have ever seen was my former hus-band Sonny Bono. He never learned to play the piano—or any other instru-ment for that matter—and some say he could barely sing. But he refused to let that stand in his way. He

would get an inspiration in the middle of the night, so he would go down to the piano and bang out a song with the only five chords he knew. Instead of ignoring it as a passing whim, he would act on it. He wrote each of his ten gold records using just those five simple chords.

If you have an inspiration you'd like to act on, start now. Once you make the commitment and decide to go for it, the energy and momentum will propel you forward. Who cares if you have no idea what you're doing? You'll just end up solving problems as they arise. Sonny believed in himself when no one else did. That is one of the greatest lessons I learned from him. **He would make a decision then jump in. If he didn't know how to swim, he'd figure it out along the way. Sonny believed in himself so powerfully that he eventually became a congressman of the United States—and mind you, he didn't even have a high school diploma!**

Style Divas always dream big and aim high. That way, even if they fall short, the experience is still pretty darn awesome!

Diva DRILL: Do It on Faith

Pick one task around your home that you've been putting off because you're convinced it won't come out right. Choose something relatively small but daunting to you. Maybe it's pruning that overgrown bush ("What if I kill it?!"), hanging a set of family photos ("What if they come out uneven? Or I crack the wall?"), or even installing a faucet that you bought that has been sitting in the box for six months now. Get started. Keep going until you've done it right, forgiving yourself ahead of time for any mistakes you make along the way (and there will be some). You'll feel great, and the confidence you build will make it easier to attack bigger projects.

head to the movies

Want to expand your style horizons? Head to the multiplex. **Movies can stir the imagination and inspire a plethora of great ideas.** Fashion designers cite films all the time as their inspiration. I personally had a tremendous affinity for the set direction in the movie *Out of Africa*. It inspired a wealth of ideas and continues to do so. I used mosquito netting in my backyard, and my drapes on the arbor were like a tent (almost like we were in the Sahara desert and needed shade). Home designers also borrow ideas from movies all the time, such as a *Lord of the Rings* theme for a child's bedroom or a modern look inspired by the movie *The Matrix*.

Sometimes the movies don't have to be particularly spectacular or even good to spark an idea. For instance, my associate Thurayya told me this fun story: In college, she took an art class in which the students went to see a famous artist and talk to him about his work. One of his most haunting paintings featured the back of a woman's head. When the artist was asked where he got his inspiration for this image, he stunned everyone by confessing that it came from the horror movie *Predator*

Diva DRILL : Video Visions

Go to a video store and judge the video by its cover art. If something hits you visually, rent it. When you get home, pop it in, and whenever a visual intrigues you—be it the treatment of the opening credits, the way the camera lingers over a landscape, or even the color of a character's shirt—make a note of it or write it in your journal. Pay attention to the way the film creates a mood through the landscapes or interiors; by the use of lighting

with Arnold Schwarzenegger. In one scene, a woman freaks out because she just saw the monster, and Arnold comments in his thick Austrian accent, **"She's out of her mind."** That line compelled the artist to paint the back of a woman's head. Later, this painting appeared in a museum, and my associate had to laugh when she heard the curator speak about it. He went on and on about how the work represented, "the intangibility of beauty and feminine shame," and how the painter was going through an important transition in his life. Everyone was happily distracted from this nonsense when Thurayya blurted out from the back, "Are you kidding me? His inspiration came from the movie *Predator*!"

One popular misconception is that in order to be truly creative and come up with brilliant ideas, you have to be "deep" and dream up fantastic visions out of thin air like an artist. That's just not how it happens. **An action movie, a late-night TV show, or a random comment can all trigger ideas if you're open to them.**

or music cues. Pause the movie to make your notes, especially if a particular shot jumps out at you and you feel you really want to take a good look at it.

After the movie, review your notes and choose the scene or image that stands out the most to you. How would you translate it into a room or space within your home? Is there a display of objects you could create based on it? Is there a color palette you might assemble to represent it? Let your imagination go and see where this one image leads you.

listen to your style voice

Your Style Diva is whispering in your ear all the time, giving you ideas and suggestions. She's a big talker! You just need to stop what you're doing sometimes and really listen to what she's trying to tell you. **Those moments of intuition are special moments that you should grab on to and never take for granted.** They're like little gems. They might seem to come at the most random times, but that doesn't make

them any less important. Something triggered it. Something made you think of it. You don't know where the thought came from. Your Style Diva is saying "Listen!"

When my inner style voice speaks to me, I always acknowledge it. That means I either act on the idea or I jot it down somewhere. **You can't ignore those moments. Otherwise, the inspiration will dissipate, and then it**

Diva DRILL : Set Aside Style Diva Time

You know full well that you can't stay in touch with your best friend, relatives, or former colleagues if you never make time to talk to them, right? Well, why do you think it's any different with your own Style Diva? Your Style Diva is an inner friend that you should listen to. Make time for her. Did you notice anything on your lunchtime walk? Was a co-worker wearing an intriguing scarf? Did you see anything while shopping? Record your Style Diva's perceptions and ideas in your Style Journal.

As you become more attuned to your Style Diva, you'll be able to hear her throughout the day. But for now, a dedicated time will help you build a strong relationship. As your Style Diva gets better at speaking up and as you get better at listening, add several other dedicated times

becomes more work to rev it up again. I get inspired every hour of the day, but I just don't have the time to create everything I dream up. Still, I try never to put stops on my ideas. They're just too valuable.

I could be creating a bedding design then, all of a sudden, have another totally different idea about candles. When that happens, **I don't drop what I'm doing and turn to the next thing (that would make me too unfocused), but I do acknowledge those inspirations and write them down somewhere so I don't forget them later.**

to "talk" with her, until you become familiar enough to hear her everywhere and anywhere. And remember to record her words of wisdom in your Style Journal whenever she speaks!

Get Inspired
POP QUIZ

Test your Get Inspired I.Q. then move on to the next section!

1   **What's the first rule of style?**

2   **What's the best way to organize your inspirational tear-sheets from magazines, books, and catalogs?**

3   **What can Mother Nature teach you about style?**

4   **When inspiration hits, what's a useful way to capture it?**

5   **If you spot an object you like while shopping, what's the first thing you should do with it?**

6   **How can you get a fresh vantage point on your present style?**

7   **Identify one childhood memory that has influenced your style.**

8   **True or false: The first idea you have is always your best.**

9   **How does clutter affect the creative process?**

10   **How can listening to your instincts help you achieve your dreams?**

Style

Color

Arrangement

Texture

Shape

Start Styling

Your inner Style Diva should be feeling a bit healthier these days, having received some inspirational nourishment and having flexed her mental muscles. Energized and enlivened by your new idea-generating regimen, she's probably feeling self-assured enough to step out of the shadows and start styling. But on what? If you're like most people, you probably don't even know where to begin.

It's time for decisions and a process. As a Style Diva, you need to move your ideas from inspiration to reality. In this section, I will introduce you to the five Senses of Style: Style, Color, Texture, Shape, and Arrangement. They are the main elements I use as a benchmark when I am styling. These senses, both individually and together, can help you evaluate why something appears stylish or why it doesn't. Your creative process will become stronger and will get you to the next level of style and confidence.

A Sense is—as the dictionary puts it—a capacity to appreciate or understand. You can begin to appreciate why one shape reflects a Modern style or another a more Classic style. Or whether a color is the right hue. If it's not, then why not?

I'll help you put these senses to use in projects that will improve your styling skills and your viewpoint towards style. We'll also talk about surrounding yourself with people who can support you. And because a positive attitude is important to being a Diva, I'll tell you how to style with boundless energy and enthusiasm! So put on a fabulous outfit, get your nails done, and let's start styling.

first things first

It all comes down to one decision: *where do you start?* **Decisions are difficult, especially when you have a lot of good options (or lots of stuff to do!), but by picking one project to focus on, you will set your styling in motion.** Otherwise, you are stuck. You'll go nowhere. You'll feel frustrated. You'll begin to wonder why you even started listening to that inner Style Diva, anyway. Make that decision!

Inspiration is wonderful. It gives us so many ideas. But that's just the problem, isn't it? Once you're open to all the style influences around you, how do you make a decision about which ones to use in your home? And how do you keep from having them all blob together into a big, confusing blur? And, for goodness sake, where on that mile-long to-do list do you actually start? Breathe, my little Style Diva, breathe! We all have a mile-long to-do list. I know firsthand what that overwhelming feeling is like.

When I have too many things to get done, I work on the easiest or smallest first. I like to feel as though I'm making progress, checking things off. Then, empowered by the sense of accomplish-

Diva DRILL : Pick a Project

Write down all the projects you want to do in your home or garden. Then, take that list and divide the projects into three categories:

1. **Mega:** projects requiring one week or more to complete, such as redoing the whole living room, landscaping the backyard, or modernizing a bath.

2. **Manageable:** projects that require about one day, for instance, laying out a buffet table for a party or planting several new containers outside.

3. **Mini:** projects that take only a few hours, for example, creating and

ment the small projects gave me, I'll go back and tackle the bigger ones!

Don't undervalue those simple styling projects that can bring immediate satisfaction. You can create a new centerpiece for the kitchen table or rearrange a shelf in your entryway. You'll get to the kitchen overhaul or the new patio soon enough. What you need right now is a focused place to start. Keep your style momentum by working on the smaller projects while the bigger ones are in progress (or while you're waiting for the resources to do them).

Once you make the decision on where to start, other decisions will come more easily. You will build off of (and exercise your style muscles with) that choice, using the five Senses of Style to help guide you. Even if your selected project is small, you're going to feel better about yourself and your space because you are moving toward a goal. **Once you've made your choice, don't waver. Get going on it, and keep going, until you've seen it through to the end. The process will be a rewarding adventure.**

hanging seasonal wreaths or arranging a centerpiece for a table.

Now, select one project from the Mini or Manageable list. Before you do anything, however, plan it out. Write the goal in your journal. Then write a list of the tasks that need to be done in order to accomplish your goal. (If you discover you have inadvertently chosen a project that's really a Mega project, move it to that list and pick another one.) Now that you've identified your project and the tasks required to do it, you'll be ready to do it with style!

name your style

Style is the first on the list of the Senses of Style. *Okay,* you're saying, *if I were comfortable with style, I wouldn't need this book!* I'm not talking about your personal style here—that's the unique stamp you put on a space, the way you dress, the way you entertain, the distinct mark that is yours. **When I say Style in the context of the five Senses of Style, I mean the overall look or sensibility you're going for in a space.** It doesn't have to be a conventional Style label (for instance: romantic, contemporary, French country, tropical), although it could be. You can come up with your own unique label such as *city sophisticate, exotic Casbah,* or *meditation sanctuary.* Use whatever label best describes it for you. Once you label it, you'll be able to see it more clearly.

Remember what I said earlier: *the first rule of style is that there are no rules.* Using a label to describe a style doesn't mean you have to conform to a narrow set of choices. **Keep in mind that the label is the *beginning* of the process, not the end.** You're coming up with your own understanding and appreciation of this style type.

There are many people who have "contemporary" living rooms. If I were to ask each of these people what "contemporary" means, one might tell me,

Diva DRILL: Create a Style Board

Get a large (24"x 36") piece of foam core board from an art supply store. Set it up in your workspace. Think about the project you've planned out in the previous Diva Drill and come up with a word or a sentence that best describes the style you want your project to have. Write it in large letters at the top of the board. Can you write it in a way that reflects the style? Riff on what that style name calls up for you, and

"A lime green and orange palette." Another might say, "Very white with clean lines." And a third person might say, "It has lots of geometric shapes and is very retro." Are these all examples of "contemporary?" Yes, but as you can see, that means very different things to different people: They use the same label, with three different visions.

Imagine that you and I are given an assignment by clients to do a "tropical backyard" makeover for their "Exotic Summer" campaign. The first question I would ask is, "What's the color palette we would use for this exotic makeover?" You might answer red, or green, or orange, or fuchsia, or tur-quoise, and all these colors would be right for a tropical style makeover. My next question would be, "What kind of plant material would we use?" You might say palms, ferns, bromeliads, gardenias, or birds of paradise. Then I would ask you, "What are some of the elements that would go into this backyard?" Let's say you answer, "Water." What kind? Running, bubbling, a fountain, a pond? A waterfall would work for this. Water running over rocks rather than a two-tiered birdbath with a statue on top? (Oooh, that sounds nice too...) No! Focus! Think "tropical." **The label you choose sharpens your focus and enables you to eliminate certain options and choose others. So, name your style type and stay focused!**

write down what that style type means to you on the board. Or try using a word processing program and choose a font that "fits" the style type to you. Write (or glue) your printed text on the board in a way that suits the style. Go through your Style File for visuals that represent this style to you; glue them to the board as well. You now have the start of a Style Board. The following Diva Drills will help you add to it.

color your world

After you choose a style type, the next most important Sense of Style is Color. In fact, some of you may already know your style so well that you use color as your launching point. **It's a key component of style because it quickly makes a statement.** It differentiates one interpretation of a style type from another, helps set a mood, and conveys personality.

My experience is that most people have an almost instinctual reaction to their favorite colors. For instance, when you go out shopping, you probably naturally gravitate towards the colors you like. It is the mixing and matching of colors that most people get hung up on. **A great deal of what makes color choices so exciting—as well as daunting—is the number of components that a color is made of.** There's *hue* (what most people think of when they think of color), *saturation* (how rich or deep the color is), and *value* or *intensity* (how bright the color is). It's the interplay between these three components that creates the infinite variety of colors around us.

How you combine these elements is what makes great color selections. You can work with only one hue and change the saturation and intensity to achieve differences between color. Want to use two different colors in a child's playroom? Try hues of the same degree of intensity, such as bright primary colors. Want to go totally 60s Mod? You could use colors that differ in all three aspects that really vibrate or pop against each other.

Which brings us to my final point. **When I'm in the mood for a new color, I change the palette as a whole; I** *don't* add little bits of different colors all over. If you add too many colors at once, it's overkill. Your eye gets pulled in too many different directions, and your style statement gets watered down. **Identify the main two colors in your palette, then add accents sparingly, introducing them lightly with just a vase, a candle accent, or one pillow and a dish on the table.**

Diva
DRILL : Swatch Watch

Go to the paint section of your local home-improvement store. Take twenty to thirty individual color strips. Choose colors you like, but don't worry whether they blend or work together. Be sure to grab a wide variety of hues: reds, purples, blues, yellows, browns, oranges, everything! Also pick up a color wheel (or print one off the Internet). You'll need it for this exercise.

Once you're at home, cut the strips into individual squares and mix them all together. Now, spread the squares out on a table and pick out the color to which you have the strongest response. Using your color wheel, pair that color with several others. First choose a shade of white that you like next to it, then one opposite from it on the color wheel (a complementary color). Now choose a color next to it on the color wheel that appeals to you (an analogous color), then a color within the original color's family. Once you have created all of these appealing pairs, choose a third color for each set using the same process.

Evaluate your sets of colors against your Style Board. Which one best speaks to your interpretation of the style? How would you use each set of three colors together? Which color would dominate? Which would be an accent? When you've made your selection, add the trio to your style board, along with notes on their use.

This is a great activity to do with your kids—especially if you're focusing on one of their rooms. You'll educate and entertain them at the same time, and you'll involve them in the styling process where they live.

89

get in touch with textures

Texture is the next of the Senses of Style. Using texture creates contrast, depth of perception, and the overall feel in a room. It is a Sense of Style that is very important to understand. Just as color helps give styles their depth, texture helps define and augment color. It enhances the tactile quality of a space, making style a thing that you can reach out and touch.

When people talk about texture, they commonly think about it in the tactile sense. For example, an item can be bumpy, smooth, coarse, jagged, velvety, or silky. However, texture can also be visual, such as shiny, glossy, or matte. You can create texture in a room by contrasting high-gloss paint on trim against the matte finish on walls.

You can use texture to create visual contrast in a room with a monochromatic color scheme. More ways to add texture that you may not have considered include: layering several picture frames on a table, placing one in front of another instead of in a line; or laying two throws one over another. Both are simple techniques for adding visual interest.

The textures you choose for a space help communicate your style. As I look around my family room, I notice

Diva DRILL: Box Yourself In

Get a shoebox and gather multiple small objects of different textures—seashells, rocks, pieces of fabric or leather, twigs, glass beads, small pieces of china or pottery, metal keys, and so forth. Place the objects in the box, sit down at a table or on the floor, blindfold yourself (or just close your eyes), and handle each of them. Pull out the ones that you respond positively to through touch. Remove your blindfold and review what you've selected. Add your choices to your Style Board. Pin or glue what you can. If the object does not lend itself to that, write down

all the different textures that come into play. The linen pillow with embroidery on my sofa sits next to a raw silk pillow and a suede and beaded pillow as an accent. In my living room, next to the sofa is an antique urn that has an earthy, rough texture. This contrasts nicely with the suede ottoman that sits close by.

My easy chair consists of sleek dark wood. Its seat is leather with a more grainy texture. Above the sofa hangs a shiny mirror trimmed in rough, natural-colored rope. All of these different elements create textures that give the room depth and interest and add to an eclectic, exotic style.

Once you have identified the Style you want in a space (see "Name Your Style"), **start thinking of the textures that match that look.** If you're going for an organic, natural style, for instance, then you might choose such fabrics as cotton, sisal, burlap, and linen to align with that sensibility. On the other hand, if you are going for an ultra-modern look, you might use very smooth textures, such as grainless leathers or highly polished metals or glass. **Even though your style may have a dominant texture theme, that doesn't mean you can't introduce a contrasting texture as an accent. In fact, you'll see that it can help make the main texture of your style more pronounced.**

a description of the texture on the board.

Whenever you're out, pick up small objects to add to this box and continue to play with what works for you. This is another great activity to do with your kids. Not only will it get your kids to understand texture, but it will also teach them (and you) to turn your attention outward. On the beach, pick up seashells or stones for the box. In the park, gather acorn caps, palm fronds, or whatever's on the ground. The more you experiment and evaluate, the better you will develop a sense of what works for you—and the whole family—in your home.

get in shape

The fourth Sense of Style is Shape. Shape is defined simply as the outline of an object. **Look all around you and observe the spectacular and diverse shapes that surround you.** When evaluating the shape of an object, it's important to study its silhouette. Take a vase, for instance. To block its texture and color from affecting your perception of it, place it with a light directly behind it so that the vase is in shadow. What do you see? Does it have a straight, smooth shape, such as a cylinder, or does it have flourishes or undulating curves? You can see the same things if you look at fashion. Take

skirts, for example. They can be full, straight, flip, or A-line. Pants can be bell-bottomed, straight-legged, or tapered. I always pay attention to shape, color, and texture when assessing how trends are moving. By doing this, you'll be able to move your style forward pretty effortlessly!

Now that you're looking at these shapes, think about how they match different styles. If you are going for a mid-century modern look, for example, you could use pure geometric shapes and clean lines. For a traditional look, you might go for outlines that are curved, detailed, or embellished—think camelback sofas and ornately carved mirrors—and avoid sleeker shapes such as square, Asian-style bowls. Shape and line can even affect choices of flower patterns. A modern look would use something like a calla lily. An English cottage look evokes images of frilled cabbage roses and peonies.

While there are no steadfast rules here, these are guidelines to help you understand how to look at shape as it relates to communicating a style.

Even without knowing how many style categories are traditionally defined, you can find the shapes that match the look you want by using information that is all around you.

Style Divas use trends to revamp their style, not to relinquish it.

Diva DRILL : Dish It Up

Studying tabletop items and decorative accessories is a great way to shape up your shape sense. Head to a home décor or department store and be sure to bring along your Style Journal! Hone in on the plates and serving pieces first. Forget about how you'd use any of the pieces; just let yourself respond to shapes that appeal to you. Make notes in your Style Journal as you go. Do round and oval items enchant you? Do the square plates have appeal? Now turn to the glasses. Which are your favorites? Short, wide tumblers or tall, narrow tea glasses? When looking at wine glasses, do you instinctively reach for round goblets or cone shapes? What about the pitchers?

Move on to decorative accessories. Do you like vases that are long and lean or trumpet-shaped or square? Grab catalogs from the design lines that you liked best.

At home, look over your notes and see which shapes you preferred. In magazines, you can find your shapes in the context of a room setting and identify what shapes best fit the overall look, or style, you want to have. Pull tear sheets from these magazines and put them on your style board to keep yourself on track for future decisions regarding shape.

arrange for a change

Arrangement is the fifth Style Sense. Arrangement refers to the way items are put together in a harmonious and balanced way. An arrangement is a composition, and what you use to compose an arrangement can include anything from furniture and flowers to plates on a table.

Arrangements, of course, pull together the other senses—style, color, texture, shape—as part of their composition. Consider a flower arrangement. You can tell a lot about a person's sense of style just by observing the way she arranges flowers. The vase, of course, introduces shape immediately. Someone leaning toward a romantic style might do a spring arrangement with a variety of different flowers—say, daffodils, muscari, and tulips. Someone preferring a simpler, bolder look might use only a single variety of flowers, like white lilies, and place them in a starkly colored vase. Balancing the form, proportion, symmetry, and space of objects in an arrangement is critical. But first things first, starting with form.

Form is the outline of the arrangement as a whole. It's what creates the impression of the arrangement as a unit. The form you use will help draw the eye to and through the items in the arrangement as well. Forms can be circular, triangular, linear, and three-dimensional. Imagine a buffet on a round dining table. You might arrange the plates in concentric circles on the table, which creates a round form horizontally, but use a tall centerpiece in the middle, which gives the table a triangular form vertically.

Symmetry happens when form and the objects within it are perfectly even and matched on both sides. Good arrangements can be symmetrical or asymmetrical. A perfectly symmetrical arrangement in which all items are paired helps to create a classical feel.

Think of chateaus in France where there might be two large urns flanking either side of a doorway, walkway, or entryway. The same look can be created in your own home with two topiaries on either side of the doorway or two vases with flowers on either side of a mantle. A tall vase on the left side of the mantle and two smaller vases on the right side would be an *asymmetrical* arrangement, but just as striking and stylish. Asymmetrical arrangements lend a more modern flair. You can use even a single object to create a composition. One large black vase set on a white shelf makes a striking, contemporary statement.

Proportion is how big or small the items are in relation to one another. Generally, you will vary the size of objects in an arrangement. (Ideally, you should have big, medium, and small objects.) But whether they are flowers, furniture, or picture frames, the bigness of one thing should be in proportion to the smallness of another, with the mid-sized object as a happy medium between the two.

Proportion is one of the toughest characteristics to judge and may require some trial and error to vary the sizes of the objects while getting the proportions balanced. For instance, if you set a tiny carved stone figurine against a huge urn, the figurine will get lost, and your arrangement will seem unbalanced.

Space is the distance around and between the objects in an arrangement. The next time you put two things in an arrangement, look at how much space you've left between them. Are they so spread out that the arrangement doesn't hold together as a unit? **Try grouping things together tightly for a change.** Hang picture frames almost touching each other or group three vases so that their shapes overlap or pack a bunch of roses into a low mint-julep cup so that the blooms form a single mass.

Now, let's talk about the type of arrangement that causes so much anxiety: furniture. I move the furniture around in my house all the time! While you may be limited in where you can put the piano or sofa in the living room, or against what wall your king-sized bed can go, you've got plenty of other items to play with in your rooms. **Take a good look at the shape, size, and proportions of the furniture as well.** For instance, pairing two small, delicate chairs with a bold linear sofa isn't going to work, no matter where you put

them. Try moving the chairs to another room and bringing in chairs that are more in proportion to the sofa.

Or maybe you're having another proportion distortion: Is all the furniture too large for the room itself, making it feel cramped and crowded (and explaining why you can't find a place to move anything)? It may be time to refurnish that room. Or do you have a few small pieces floating about a large room? This case may be easier to solve. A tightly grouped furniture arrangement will give that room a center and focus.

Furniture placement is also about flow. Do you want people to move through the room quickly? Gather in a particular space? Feel relaxed and spread out, or cozy and chatty? Consider the style statement you can make by where you put the armchairs in the living room: close to the sofa for an intimate, conversational space; farther back, against the wall to set a more formal mood in the room. **You can influence the way people act in your rooms by how you arrange the furniture. How's that for some Diva power?**

Style Divas are allowed to change their minds... over... and over...

and over... again!

Diva DRILL : Get a Move on It

Rearrange the furniture in your living room to create three separate arrangements. If you can't move the sofa, focus on what you can easily move—chairs, the coffee table, side tables, lamps, large vases, or decorative objects. Live with each arrangement for at least one or two days—sitting on each piece of furniture, reading, walking around—and record in your Style Journal what works and what doesn't work about each arrangement.

Is there a piece that doesn't fit no matter where you put it? How does the flow of the room change? Have you found a new, interesting focal point in the room? When you find one that really works, make a map of the room and pin it to your Style Board.

shady business

Lighting and shade, while not a Sense of Style, help you finish off a room or space. **How you light a room helps convey a mood.** The same room can be bright and cheery or romantic or cozy—or, unfortunately, dull and depressing—all depending on how you light it. That's not to say shade or shadow is bad. Both the presence and absence of light can help create moods. Think of a romantic, candlelit dinner. The intimate glow of the candles creates a space that draws two people closer. Light filtering through to a hammock under palm trees can lend a feeling of serenity, escape, and peacefulness.

Light and shade can create a feeling of warmth or coolness. Great artists know this. The "Houses of Parliament" series by French impressionist Claude Monet is a dramatic example. He painted the exact same scene from his window four times, at different times of the day, and in different seasons, achieving stunning but hugely different works each time.

When I work with lighting, I study the natural light first then make decisions on how to add to or subtract

Diva DRILL: Get in the Mood

Choose a room or space in your home. In your Style Journal, write down the mood you'd like represented there—romantic, welcoming, energizing, serene. Describe what that word means to you personally. Finally, begin adding notes on what kind of light and shadow give you that feeling. Do you find serenity, for instance, in places that are bright and cool? Warm and shaded?

Now, spend one day recording what the light, both natural and interior, is like in your home at different times of the day. Visit it in the morning, midday, late afternoon, and night. How has the light

from it to create the mood I want. For instance, if I'm styling a room to be the energetic center of the house, I'll look at how the light comes in at different times of the day. Maybe it has a beautiful, filtered light in the morning but gets a lot, even too much, in the mid-afternoon and then is too dark at night. Using both interior lights and window treatments, I'll balance the room so that it has a more consistent mood throughout the day. Billowy, sheer curtains let the morning light in but block some of the blinding afternoon sun. By adding bright lamps or ceiling lights, I keep the room feeling alive even at dusk.

You can also use this technique to give rooms very different moods at various times of the day. A family room that's bright and cheery due to daytime sun can be made warm and cozy at night by closing floor-length curtains and turning on lamps to create warm tones.

changed? Perhaps you like the light at one time of day but not another. The kitchen, for instance, makes you feel *happy* in the morning, but come dinnertime, you find it cold and unwelcoming. Note what happens if you change things throughout the day. Pull a shade off one of the lamps in your living room, or throw a sheet over a window in your bedroom when the sun is the brightest.

If you have trouble achieving the effect you want with natural light only, the problem may be that you don't have enough interior lighting or the right type of lights to give a room the feeling you want. Hit the hardware store to buy some light bulbs. Choose ones of different wattages and different "temperatures," such as soft white, rose, or amber.

from sense to sensibility

As you've developed your Style Senses, you've been noting which colors, shapes, and textures inspire you and align with your interpretation of a style. But you may still feel lost. **The trick is to find one particular element that will get the ball rolling.**

It might be as simple as a peacock feather! Last year, I traveled around the country to various retail stores, showing customers how to style their tabletops with an exotic flair. We would arrive at the store with no props. We'd then walk through the aisles pulling items that were right for our table setup. We never knew what we'd find from store to store.

One time during the holiday season, we arrived at a store to set up our table and found ourselves amid a sea of Christmas golds, reds, whites, and greens—seasonally appropriate, perhaps, but not exactly right for an exotic flair. We had to think fast. I sent my associate to the women's accessory department on a mission to find scarves, jewelry, hats—anything she could find to help set the tone. She returned

bearing five brightly colored scarves and peacock feathers. Peacock feathers! Genius! They were shades of turquoise and green and very exotic. Those feathers were the perfect inspirational element to set our table in motion.

I took one of the scarves that was in a similar color palette and laid it as a runner. I fanned the peacock feathers out on a cake pedestal in the center of the table. I recalled seeing turquoise bulbs in the ornament section and dashed off to get those. I filled a glass bowl with turquoise and green holiday bulbs and set it on the cake stand. We added tall glass vases to continue the bold statement through shape, along with exotic flowers that the caterer provided.

The element you choose should spark your creativity and set the whole project in motion. If it's the right object, it can determine your style. The peacock feather's color palette (deep, rich turquoise with green and sapphire

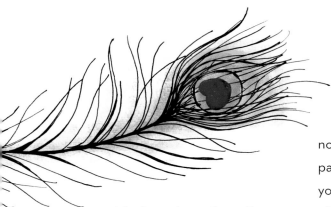

blue), its shape (long, flowing, dramatic), and its texture (iridescent) all portrayed the exotic style I was trying to create. From there, I continued building with other accessories, arranging them in bold, dramatic ways.

There were things I specifically chose not to use, and that's an equally important part of using your Senses of Style. When you're creating an arrangement, don't be afraid to subtract as well as add. You might try an object with the right style but find it has the wrong color for your arrangement. Or it might have the right style and shape, but wrong texture. **Keep your eyes open (and Senses attuned) to what's not working as well as what is.**

Diva DRILL: Get Centered

Imagine you have to do an entertaining table using only what you have in your house. Choose whatever style you wish—modern, holiday, classic, vintage. Begin by deciding what object (or objects) will go in the center of the table. Just be sure that the object represents the style you're going for. Maybe it's a crystal vase you'll fill with flowers or fruits; maybe it's a tall, freestanding wood carving from Africa.

Next, choose your table covering. Let this and your center object set the color palette, textures, and shapes of the rest of your display. Add candles, serving dishes, and decorative objects by considering the colors, textures, and shapes that work with your initial object *and* continue to communicate your concept. If you have gone with the African carving, then maybe you bring in more wood bowls and pottery pieces. If your style is elegant vintage, you could use tarnished silver pieces (you don't have to eat on them but they have more character). Crystal stemware and maybe some pink-hued accents can enhance the look.

Arrange and rearrange until—voila! You've made your style a reality!

put your home **on a diet!**

Have you ever looked at a room and thought, "Where did all this stuff come from?" Well, I'll tell you: Somebody brought you a birthday gift and you put it on the table. You found a new pillow that you loved and you added it to a chair. You bought a new vase, brought it home, and put it by a lamp. You found a great picture frame at a swap meet. **Over time, stuff begins to accumulate, and next thing you know, your home is overweight and bloated**.

This happens to everyone—even the most advanced Style Diva. The reason? We like to add, not subtract. We like to eat, not diet! We don't like restrictions, and the more stuff the better! It's just not natural (is it?) to throw away something that's "perfectly good" even if you don't wear it or need it! The truth is, all those "extras" weigh your style down.

If you want to build style confidence and see your home in a new way, you're going to need to lose some excess weight. In home terms, this means clearing the clutter—even just temporarily—to get a whole new perspective.

When I'm working on a room—either in my own home or someone else's—the first thing I do is remove everything I can—all the decorative accessories, pillows, throws, and small objects and put them on the floor or on a table to the side. Once all those items are cleared, I can see the room again, and I have a fresh canvas to work with. I will start anywhere that inspires me. Generally, that means with the bigger pieces.

In my living room, for example, I always start with the pillows on the sofa; they anchor my color palette. Then I move across the room to the mantle, which is opposite the sofa, and then over to the piano at the end of the room, and finally to the coffee table. By working in this manner, **I create the largest focal points first and use them to set the tone, color, and style in the room.**

Now that you've slimmed down your room, you're probably wondering what to do with all those extra accessories. Good question! You could toss them out or have a garage sale, but if these items have sentimental value, just put them in a storage place where the contents are easily accessible and organized.

Some people like to sort their extra decorative accessories by style. I do this and then further categorize by color. In one cabinet, I have all my exotic items and wood pieces. In a large, open cabinet I have my glass vases and plates and candles by color. In another, I keep all my pillows; in yet another, my linens. This way, I can open up a cabinet and quickly get inspiration to style with a specific palette.

Diva DRILL : Review, Reduce, Remove

Choose one display cabinet or shelf to pare down. Remove everything you've accumulated there and put all your stuff in another room or at the far end of the same room. Pick three objects that speak to the style you're going for—that have the shapes, the colors, and the textures that represent the look you're building on your Style Board.

Did you review all your old objects and discover that *nothing*—or maybe only one thing—corresponds to your new vision? Time to say goodbye to some things. Pack it all up; don't try to force square pegs (or vases or picture frames) into round holes. With your space, as well as your mind, cleared, go out shopping for the three things you'll use to turn that display area into a style statement.

wardrobe your home

If you think about it, fashion and home décor lead parallel lives. **What may be hot in the fashion world last year carries over to the home world the next year.** When I use words like embroidery, sequins, and layers, I could be talking about what's inside your closet or about soft home décor. For this reason, one wonderfully innovative way to think about styling your home is to imagine yourself giving it a new wardrobe. Just like you buy new shoes to update your look, you can do the same to your home by adding a few funky pillows. Or just as you might mix and match certain colors in your evening wear, why not do the same in your living room?

Take a close look at the clothes hanging in your closet—this is style idea central. Do you favor funky, vintage clothes? Southwestern outfits in tones of sand and blue, coupled with big, Mexican, silver and turquoise accessories? Cleanly styled, classic suits? Are your skirts full or straight? Are you into cotton or cashmere? Leather or lace? Now, make a mental note of your personal style in terms of fashion. From there, ask yourself what fabrics, colors, and styles in your wardrobe might transfer to your home. If your fashion sense is eclectic, you may opt to mix fabrics and textures in your living space and include an interesting combination of unique items. If you're more conservative, you may be comfortable in a home that's more classic and tailored.

But even as you have a set style in clothes and home décor, you still need a variety of options. Just as you have shirts, pants, and sweaters in different colors, you should also have a wide spectrum in towels, sheets, decorative pillows, and dinnerware. This gives you more options and more flexibility to mix and match according to the mood you want to set, the type of party you're throwing, or even the season. You've got at least two outfits to wear out to dinner, right? As a parallel, I recommend that you have two or three different sets of dinnerware. One of them should be a neutral color, like cream or white, that you can combine with different color palettes and accents, just as you have black pants or skirts that go with pretty much anything.

Don't think that in order to create a new décor you should only purchase new items. Again, let your wardrobe be your guide. You wouldn't buy a completely new wardrobe for spring, but you probably would buy a few new pieces to complement what you already have. Same principle goes for your home. Use what you already have, but freshen up your look with new accents. These could be candles, vases, comforters, sheets, pillows, throws, table runners. **The idea is to give your home a makeover without making a major investment.**

Diva DRILL : Accessorize Exercise

While I'm not one for rules, as you know, there's a great deal of truth to the clothing-fashion adage that teaches us: If you can't overhaul your wardrobe to match the trends, you can update your accessories. Now you're going to put this maxim into play for your home! Head out to purchase three to five new accessories for your home that would make it feel up-to-date.

Whether you head to a favorite store or try a new destination, keep your eye out for what's fresh this season. Look for bath towels, a vase or display bowl, a throw or pillows, candles, even glass pebbles in a current color to put in a clear container. Choose things you could put out immediately when you get home to freshen things up.

Even if you favor a traditional style, a good shopping trip will show you that there are plenty of options. You'll find designers are always reinterpreting looks— even the traditional—using current colors, textures, and shapes. This makes it easy to freshen the look of a home without rethinking your entire interior.

make the most with what you have

One year I decided to get my Christmas tree at the end of November. **I figured if I was going to spend this much time getting my place together for the holidays I should be able to enjoy it for at least six weeks.** I spent hours picking out the perfect tree. Should I go with a Fraser Fir, a Douglas Fir, a Balsam Fir, or a Colorado Blue Spruce? Usually I choose a Blue Spruce because I love the powdery blue needles, but that year I opted for a Douglas Fir because I spotted one that was unusually full.

The next day, I got a call from the *Today* show, asking me to come to New York to do a style segment. After being gone for four days, I was shocked to find on my return that my magnificent tree was on its last legs. It had turned a dusty blue-gray (should have gotten that blue spruce after all), and its long, beautiful branches now sagged like a weeping willow. As I looked at the tree in disbelief, I noticed the sun's rays beaming in through the skylights and floor-to-ceiling windows. Oops! I had filled the basin with water, but it was bone dry. The sun had killed the tree in just four days!

What was I to do with this dead Christmas tree? Leave it out on the curb for the trash collectors five weeks before Christmas? My neighbors knew what I did for a living. What would they think of me now? Talk about bad public relations! I decided that I better keep it and just try to make the best of it.

Diva DRILL : Sofa Makeover

Imagine that your sofa has a stain or that a child put his chocolate-covered fingers on the cushions or that your dog jumped up on the sofa with his wet paws. (Okay, maybe this doesn't take so much imagination!) You've tried washing it and spraying it, but you can't get the stains out. Guests are coming in an hour, and you have to do something quick. What

I looked at the pathetic tree and thought I better figure out a way to lift those lifeless branches. I went into my studio hoping for some inspiration. On one of my shelves was a pile of unused grapevine wreaths that I'd bought for my television segment. Unwinding the wreaths, I wrapped the grapevines around and around the tree. *Voila*—an immediate improvement. The support improved the shape, and the vines gave some texture.

Next, I used ribbon to hang some large cinnamon sticks, pinecones, and gold bulbs. I complemented them with anything else I could find in that earth-tone color palette. I then ran out and bought some fresh-seeded eucalyptus, silver dollar eucalyptus, and juniper berry branches and started sticking them in the tree, hoping to give it some fresh life and fresh scent! When I finished, I stood back and looked at my handiwork and decided it was actually acceptable. It wasn't what I'd imagined my tree would look like a week ago, but I was quite exhilarated that I had salvaged it and maybe no one would be the wiser!

Sometimes the creative problems that you face set you in a direction that you might not expect. By having to make the best of a situation, you train your mind to go through a creative process that's completely new and unexpected. There have been many Christmas trees since, but believe it or not, that grapevine tree has gone down in history with my family members as one of their favorites! It was a Style Diva victory.

would a Style Diva do? Think about throws, bed covers, and fabrics that you could use. Would quickly changing the lighting help? Don't let yourself get overwhelmed when the unexpected happens. There's almost always something that can be done with a little ingenuity.

get focused

When you walk into your living room, where does your eye go? Does it go anywhere, everywhere, or nowhere? Does it make you feel scattered when you enter? If it does, you probably haven't created any focal points in the space. Often I'll walk into a home and discover a lot of cute little decorative accessories like glass figurines and objets d'art—scattered around the room.

There's nothing calling my attention when I enter the room, nor can I put together what the occupant is trying to tell me with her things. It's all just *stuff*. And it's *everywhere*.

Your rooms should be like an unfolding story, beginning with the big statement made by the main focal point and then continuing through the use of secondary arrangements—smaller items deliberately grouped together to tell a story. These are called "vignettes," and each is anchored by its own focal point. Some rooms have natural focal points. For example, architectural elements such as a mantel or large bay window. Sometimes it's up to you to make one.

The stories your rooms tell may be literal stories—such as one told by a collection of art brought back from exotic travels—or they may be stories about color, shape, and texture. Just

A Style Diva loves "stuff"— as long as it's not in her way.

as random lines jotted all over a page don't make a story in a book, random little objects scattered all around don't make a story in a room. You have to consider what you are trying to tell the viewer with each arrangement. Perhaps it's a meditation on color, achieved through the use of objects of contrasting textures and shapes all in the same hue. Perhaps it's a family history, told through a tightly spaced, asymmetrical display of generational portraits. **Whatever it is, make sure you have a bold, strong focal point that creates a place to start and that you stick to your story line!**

Ironically, I find that people often have a hard time creating a visual story for some of their most treasured objects, such as family heirlooms or mementos. They could be baby shoes that you received at the hospital the day your child was born, or an old picture frame from grandma. You may feel uncertain about trying to mix them with other small items, or around a bigger item that steals all the attention. How do you make items like this more prominent? One Style Diva secret is to use a glass cabinet as a mini-museum to display these special items and make a statement with your memories.

If you don't have a cabinet like this, you'll just need to flex your creative muscle a little. For example, you can put your sentimental items in a picture frame or shadow box. I love collecting belts and have quite a large collection from India, Mexico, Guatemala, Greece, and other locales. Some are gold, some are silver, others are handmade by artisans with feathers and beads and stones. I love these belts, and I consider them a collection, yet they mostly collect dust

or take up space in my drawer. So I decided to choose my favorite ones and frame them in clear, Plexiglass display boxes, which I then hung in the hallway. They made a huge style statement and

went from being mere belts to pieces of art that many could admire!

Creating a main focal point for a room may be as simple as doing a dramatic, bold floral arrangement and setting it out in the main visual space of the room. I am always looking for plant material from the outdoors to cut and bring indoors. For instance, I like to place long, gorgeous, fresh peach branches in full blossom in a vase in my living room. As you work with floral displays, always be thinking about bold statements of color, shape, size, or texture.

Diva DRILL: Shadow Boxing

A good way to learn how to showcase small items together boldly is to create shadow boxes. Visit an art-supply or framing store to get a shadow box that matches your chosen style. At home, gather up small keepsakes of a given theme—shells and rocks the kids have collected from the beach, mementos from a beloved great-aunt, old vinyl record albums and other music memorabilia, even holiday items. From your treasure trove, choose one item to be the focus of your design, and set it into the shadow box. Now, begin adding other related items, reworking the arrangement in the shadow box as you go, until you have an arrangement that makes a strong statement. To keep the display from getting too cluttered or to make a decision about some of the items you're putting in, step back from the box as you work, viewing from about the distance one would view it when it's on display. When you've finished, permanently affix everything inside and hang or display it on its own. (And put away or get rid of the stuff you didn't use!) Create additional boxes using other items, perhaps one box for each of your children's rooms, using the process to create bold statements and to clear out the clutter of objects around the house.

pick a style buddy

One of the great secret weapons of all Style Divas is the styling buddy—somebody whose taste aligns with yours, somebody whom you can bounce ideas off of, and somebody who challenges you in a positive way. You don't choose this person because she is your best friend or because she excels at home design or gardening. You choose a style buddy because she is in sync with your style sensibility, loves the same stores, or has a similar passion for the creative process (although her style doesn't have to be the same). Your style buddy must also share your level of enthusiasm and energy because you don't want them to burn out midway through a shopping spree while you're just getting started. That's a styling bummer!

My styling buddy is my dear friend Brian. He's a well respected stylist who works on photo shoots for major magazines and companies and someone who has worked on my television show. We can go out all day shopping and never run out of gas. We have so much fun. We stroll down aisle after aisle, stopping to look at furniture, touching dishes, talking about the latest trends. We share the same style sensibility and have total respect for each other's opinions.

A good styling buddy challenges

Diva DRILL : Find a Style Buddy— or Several!

In your Style Journal, write down a list of attributes your ideal style buddy would have. Does he or she love to cook, like modern or Asian style, or really know fabrics? Now, review this list to identify whom you might go shopping with regularly. You might find one person who can encompass all the things you're looking for, or several pals who each have their own strengths: one who is great with clothes and furniture;

you to look at your decisions in a fresh way. Who wants a shopping buddy who agrees with you all the time? You want somebody to open your imagination to new concepts, new ideas, and new questions. Brian does this for me, and I do the same for him. We have no secret agenda, no battle of the egos. **We don't always agree, but we constantly bounce new ideas and inspirations back and forth, and this process expands both of us creatively.**

Style Divas can hear your opinion but are not always at liberty to listen to you.

another who is totally into cookware, crafts, and housewares; a third who has an incredible way with flowers, indoors and out.

Before you hit the stores, bring your selected buddy through your home or garden, show your style board, and so on. This way, if she sees something while she's out with you, or even comes across something on her own, she can tell you. Then ask her to go shopping with you!

shop like a pro

In the "Get Inspired" section, I had you go on an inspiration mission, in which you visited your favorite stores, not to purchase anything, but strictly to get ideas. I know that was pure torture. Sorry! Now you get to put your shopping groove on and head out to buy specific items, preferably with your style buddy in tow.

Obviously, in my line of work, I do quite a bit of shopping and I'm always on the lookout for cool items that work with my style. **But here's a secret the pros know: We don't always buy new stuff. The even bigger secret is that we are always on the lookout for a bargain!** We shop at garage sales, thrift stores, flea markets and the like all the time. For twenty dollars, I bought a wonderful old tapestry piece at the Rose Bowl flea market that I then threw over a table for an instant style update. Sometimes you have to weed through a lot of trash to find such treasures, but they're out there!

As a result of doing this for years, I've come up with some tips and tricks that might help you save money, time, and your sanity. Below is a list of items you should always keep an eye out for, and why.

Fabric: You'd be amazed how often you can find remnants, even bolts, of fabric at garage or estate sales. I keep a plastic bin full of odd pieces of fabric with my styling supplies (by color of course) because they come in handy all the time. You can use odd pieces of fabric in many ways: to drape an entry table, line a serving tray, re-cover an old lamp shade, or layer with other pieces to form a tablecloth. Find a large enough piece and you may be able to re-cover some furniture!

Tapestries or old drapes:
You are likely to find that these items are very inexpensive, so snatch them up. These will have many uses. You can drape them behind a bed as a faux headboard, hang them on a wall as a piece of art, or use them in place of a tablecloth to lend texture or an old-world feel to the room. The possibilities are endless.

Silver pieces: Pick up odd pieces of silver flatware, bowls, vases, or platters and start a collection. The more mismatched, the better! Honestly, I think you should buy any piece of silver that you find at a great price. Any one of them makes a great addition to your style collection. (And if it's not something you can use, then it makes for a fantastic gift!) Don't worry about tarnish; a nice patina makes it all the more stylish.

Old furniture: Look for timeworn tables, chairs, chests, stools, and lamp bases. Any of these items can be recycled, repainted, refinished, or re-covered. Just adding a random piece can lend character to a room.

Garden accessories: Dig through the pile for buckets, bins, tins, rakes, old ladders, wagons, and fence pieces. Ladders can be used as plant stands, buckets as containers for cut flowers, and wagons as planters in the back of your garden. Whether you use them inside or out, year-round or only seasonally, they add a touch of style.

Diva DRILL: The Fifty-Dollar Challenge

Get a bunch of friends together and visit a local thrift store, flea market, or garage sale. Play a game: Set an amount you each have to spend (say twenty-five or fifty dollars) to find the most stylish stuff possible. It can be one item or a collection of items. The goal is to buy with style in mind (use your Senses of Style!) and to prove that you don't have to have thousands of dollars to find stylish goods.

that's **what friends** are for

Some projects are just too big to do on your own, and perhaps hiring dozens of contractors just isn't in your budget. So how are you going to get the job done? In case I haven't made this completely clear yet, let me say it straight out: **as a Style Diva you don't have to go at it alone.** Yes, a Style Diva listens to her instincts and inspi- rations, but she knows how to ask for help and give it as well. **So why not ask your friends for help?**

We all know people who are ex- perienced at different home improvement projects: painting, plant- ing, hanging wallpaper, or organizing. A person doesn't have to do these professionally to be good at it, and sometimes you just need an extra hand!

Trading favors can help many people. Perhaps your best girlfriend has just ended a relationship and needs some help getting rid of all the reminders of her former boyfriend or husband. Head over to her place and help her weed through the stuff and pack up the boxes she can't face. Next weekend, she can help you hang drapes. Or maybe your neighbors have been renovating their house on their own. Offer them some of your time to paint the kitchen, and next month ask them for help going to the tile store to help you bring it all back and unload it. Most people have a skill they enjoy or a task they don't mind doing (it could be something you normally dread). **Just by asking, you may be surprised at how much you and your friends and neighbors can do for each other. Don't forget to make time to return the favor!**

116

Style Divas aren't afraid to ask for help in order to make their visions a reality.

Diva
DRILL : Start a Stylin' Swap

Identify a few friends or close acquaintances whom you can gather together on the weekends for some styling. Pick people whom you trust and whose company you enjoy, of course. Book regular times to work on each others' projects. You can "trade" spaces—maybe one week you work on your garden together; the next weekend you go over to a friend's house to help paint her family room. At the end of the day, have dinner together to celebrate and relax. It's a great way to bond and share something creative together.

field an all-star style team

While I truly believe in trading favors with friends and neighbors, I need to let you in on a little secret:

sometimes you need a professional! Behind every great Style Diva is a great team of professionals, lending their

assistance and expertise to the cause. I call them the All-star Style Team.

Style Teams come in two different forms. First is the **Home Team**. These are all the pros who come to your house to help you out. Your MVP (most valuable player) is your handyman, who can fix, repair, and install all the little things that were holding you back. Some of you are lucky enough to live with this person. For everyone else, be prepared to hire one when necessary.

A handyman changes lightbulbs in areas you couldn't reach, hangs drapes, fixes the broken kitchen cabinet, or hangs paintings so they're earthquake (and toddler) proof. He's indispensable to your sanity, and by the time he leaves, you'll wonder how you ever survived without him. Don't be discouraged if you have had failures with handymen before, or if you don't find the right person the first time. And when you go into a store, don't be embarrassed to introduce yourself to the

manager and let him know what project you are working on. You'd be surprised how many good handyman references I have received that way.

Another vital team member is the gardener. This could be a regular gardener who does all of your landscape planting and maintenance or someone who comes once or twice a year to handle heavy seasonal cleanups, fertilize the lawn, spray for pests, and do a good once-over on the bushes. For all the makeovers in my show *Surprise Gardener*, I had the **Green Team,** which swooped in to raise gravel, turn soil, plant beds, and hang plants—all in one day. We never could have done it without them. Need a good gardener? A good, locally owned garden center or nursery is going to know the best ones in the area.

A good carpenter is another valuable addition to your team, offering help with small or big jobs, from fixing doors to building cabinets. Also

important are a good painter and upholsterer. Sometimes it's worth it to hire a professioinal for difficult jobs. Again, you want individuals who are trustworthy and reliable. Local vendors can almost always refer you to the best in your area.

Next up is the **Away Style Team**. These are all the local merchants who run businesses outside your home that are vital to your success. I've already told you I value these folks for their handyman referrals. I also treasure them for their product knowledge and ability to do the hunting and gathering for me.

Say you're making a tablecloth and want a textured fabric that's also washable and inexpensive. A good fabric store clerk can not only help you cull through what's in stock but can also call in other samples or watch for new materials as they arrive. It works the same way with paint store employees. They can help you choose colors, answer questions, give advice on bases and finishes, and guide you through the sometimes confusing world of color. A good hardware store employee is also essential. For my local merchants, I generally choose mom-and-pop stores rather than the big chains. **It's easier to establish a relationship in such a store because the personnel turnover is less—and if you develop a rapport with the manager or owner, you will get even more personalized attention.**

Diva DRILL : Create Your Home Style Team

Develop a card file of five to ten handymen, craftspeople (upholsterers, furniture restorers), and contractors (electricians, plumbers, carpenters, painters). Use referrals from local merchants, visit local home expos, and talk to friends and neighbors. Make calls to references and identify who might work best with your style and budget. Then, as small projects arise, have these folks do the work for you. You'll eventually have the right team to play with larger projects. Keep track of projects that different people have worked on for you—and remember to give referrals for people you've liked. They'll be extra eager to do good work for you if they know you're a source for other jobs.

Build a similar file of merchants, too. When it comes to stores, it pays to make yourself a "regular." When you go to shops you like, get to know the owner, the manager, and the sales associates. Get their cards and give them your name and contact info. Tell them what you're looking for, as well as what you liked in the store. Ask them to be on the lookout so that when fabulous new stuff comes in, you're the first one they call.

camouflage techniques

I try to keep some semblance of predictability in my daily life, but sometimes—okay, most times—this doesn't work out. In my line of work, I have to be ready for last-minute surprises, and sometimes that means sixty people showing up in a few hours.

A few years ago, the producers for *Outer Spaces* wanted to throw a wrap party for the entire crew. When the restaurant arrangements fell through on the day of the party, I volunteered my own home. As soon as I hung up the phone, **I looked around and realized I had two hours to get my place ready for sixty guests!** There was no time to worry about it. I had to snap into action.

The first question I asked my-

Diva DRILL: Create a Cover Up

The next time a last-minute gathering brews a storm on your style horizons, meet the challenge with a cover-up. Look at how you can use lighting to disguise the flaws of your space. Perhaps your new romantic interest is coming over and the place is a mess. Push everything you can into the corners and use dim lights and strategically placed candles to keep the focus on the center of the room—and on you and your

self was, "Where am I going to put everyone?" My living room was too small. I decided the pool area was perfect because it could fit everyone. But, oh boy, the surrounding yard was not quite in the shape I would have liked it to be in for sixty guests! I'd been shooting for weeks and hadn't had time to deadhead plants, freshen up any of the pots with annuals, or restyle the area. The gardener wasn't due for several days, and there were dead, dried leaves everywhere. I barely had time to sweep up and get a table laid out before the whole crew of my show was on their way. (An outdoor living show!) Holy hibiscus, what would they think of me?!

I had closets stuffed with candles, and this was an evening party. A match made in heaven! I lined the walls around the pool, the driveway, and the tables with fifty votives and tea lights in little groups of three or four. The twinkling lights created a magical glow, which masked all the imperfections in my yard.

It's amazing what a little spontaneous creativity and fifty candles can do.

On the set the next day, people raved about the "mood" and the "spirit" of the evening. All I was trying to do was hide the state of the yard! Sometimes a certain styling technique forced on you by necessity will be the thing that is the most memorable. When that happens, take note and recreate it again and again.

fabulous Diva dress. Last-minute dinner plans at your place and no time to get a flower arrangement together? Create a centerpiece using candles of varying heights and shapes. Has a rainstorm-induced power outage threatened to put out the lights on the plans for your son's birthday party? Light a huge fire and have everyone over anyway—and maybe change the menu to fire-roasted hot dogs and marshmallows.

act like a child

When I find myself stuck on a project or overwhelmed by all the demands of a job, I think of my six-year-old daughter, Hailey. She approaches everything she does with such freedom of expression. Her world is one of unlimited imagination and confidence. She's already a Style Diva extraordinaire (with four wardrobe changes a day), and she's only in first grade!

Adopting the attitude of a child is a wonderful practice in all creative endeavors. As we get older and seemingly wiser, we end up being a bit more concerned about how we are perceived by others. We become rigid, too comfortable in our ways, or fearful of pushing limits. A child has none of these concerns. She's completely free and fearless. A child would never say, "I don't know how to do this." She may not be an architect, but she has no problem making sandcastles in her sandbox. Your son may not have a real horse or

Diva DRILL: Play Dress Up with the Dinner Table

Have you ever watched children put together outfits for their imaginary games? Do the same with your indoor or outdoor dining area. Get out all your tablecloths, serving pieces, dishes, glassware—everything you own for entertaining—and put all the items near your dining table. Now, imagine you're setting the table for a very formal party or a Wild-West barbecue or a fairy's garden outside. As you go, search for other non-tabletop objects to add. For instance, would you

a saloon, but he manages to play Cowboys and Indians, and it's real to him.

Sometimes I'll take Hailey to garage sales, and I'll say, "Let's see if we can find some things to add to your tea party set." There might not be a teapot or cups in sight, but that doesn't stop her mind from dreaming up all sorts of new and fabulous uses for random items. She'll pick up a small vase or a napkin or even a cute figurine that would look great on the table. She teaches me. She gets me to use my imagination and let it run free.

When you approach style like a child, you expand your creative repertoire. Through my play with Hailey, I look at items differently. I try to really think how an item can be used in a new way. **If you really want to keep your own imagination nimble, ask yourself the quintessential child's question: "Why?"** Kids don't take anything for granted. They don't know the "rules," and so they don't limit themselves. **And that is the essence of being a Style Diva.**

Style Divas can see treasure in other peoples' trash

tie straw hats to chairs to create a garden party theme? Which objects work when paired for this theme, although you might not normally put them together? Ask your children to come and play, too. Watch what they choose, and follow their imaginative inspirations. And hey, if you end up having a fairy garden tea party at the end, enjoy it!

strut like a style diva

I'm not going to lie to you: being a Style Diva isn't always a walk in the park (though we do enjoy those for inspiration). But part of the joy of styling is enjoying the process. **In order to be a Style Diva, you have to assume the part.** That means adopting a positive, enthusiastic, can-do attitude that says to the world, "I'm going to start this, I'm going to finish this, and I'm going to love the entire journey to get there." Whatever stylish project a Style Diva embarks on, she knows there will be problems and barriers along the way. She accepts those challenges, and she's not afraid to face them. In fact, she looks forward to it. **Because here's the thing: A Style Diva loves the creative process as much as she loves the end result.**

You would never hear a Style Diva say, "I'll be happy once my house is finished" because, to her, it's never "finished." It's always evolving, as her life does. Think about it. When you look back, it's the process that is full of memories and it's the overcoming of barriers while you are getting there that makes you feel good, not just the results.

I'll never forget the time I got a call from an editor at a newspaper saying, "We want to do a photo shoot of your outdoor patio two days from now so it makes it into the Sunday paper." They had already shot the backyard once, so it couldn't look the same. I happily accepted the offer, even though I had no time. This called for a backyard style blitz!

I called in my staff, and we cleaned up plants, moved stuff around, pruned, and watered. Then I ran out to the store and picked up a bunch of new decorative pillows in blue teal with green stripes for my outdoor furniture. Although this wasn't my usual color palette, teal was in style at that time, and I thought it would be a fun change. I also picked up a bunch of seashells, candles, and a mirror. When I got back to my home, I arranged and rearranged everything. But something was still not right. One side felt incomplete, as if an important piece were missing. What was it? I looked up towards the sky, and there was a boring, beige umbrella covering the table. I suddenly realized that was the problem. It needed color to tie it all together.

I remembered a cabana veil in netting that I had bought a year ago and never used. I could use this to cover the umbrella. Only one problem: the netting was white. That was not going to work for this project (not enough color).

I really wanted teal. It was the night before the shoot, but once I had the idea it was hard to shake it. **Style Divas love challenges,** so off I went to the drug store where I purchased some Rit dye. When I got home, I realized I hadn't dyed anything since tie-dyeing T-shirts in my teenage days. This was going to be interesting. I experimented on a few towels, mixing greens and blues in the sink, failing time and time again. I didn't panic; I just continued, knowing that it would all work out.

Finally I got the color just right and matched it up with the pillow. I was ecstatic, and it couldn't have been more right if I had gone out to purchase it. I dropped into bed around midnight very proud of my style victory. **Yes, even a Style Diva should be proud of her accomplishments.**

Diva D R I L L : Refresh Yourself

The next time you're in the middle of a project—hanging pictures, clearing out a cluttered bookshelf, or painting a room—and the work is going slower than you thought, or you feel it'll never come out right, go take a break. Pour a cool glass of ice tea and sit down with your Style Journal, Style File, and Boards. Get back in touch with why you're doing this in the first place. Clear your head of what's taking so long or not going right. Now go back to the space and reevaluate what you're working on and see how one idea can lead to another. Wait—you've made progress! Oh yeah, this was a disaster a few hours ago, and now it's on its way. See what a change of pace can do?

start a style scrapbook

"Before and after." You have heard this expression many times from me as I have taken you through make-over after makeover on television. As you proceed along the path of Style Divadom you want to be sure to document all your challenges and victories, too. That's why I recommend put-

ting together a Style Scrapbook. This photographic tribute to all your styling accomplishments will forever capture rooms you've redone, gifts you've made, gardens you've transformed, and parties you've thrown. **Don't worry** how dramatic a project it is. **Don't worry** if it's just a little tweak. **Don't**

Diva DRILL: A Night to Remember

You've probably made scrapbook pages of many parties. But how often do you include the table setting? Beginning with the Senses of Style you've been working with (style, color, texture, shape, arrangement), plus lighting considerations, experiment with doing the

worry if it's not the best thing you've ever done. **What's important is that you snap a picture of it and pop it in your scrapbook.**

The value of a Style Scrapbook is two-fold. First, you're acknowledging to yourself and the world that you've created something. By collecting your work in a book, it makes your accomplishments tangible, concrete, and meaningful. No longer are they just fading memories—they're captured in time for all to see.

Second, a Style Scrapbook will lift your spirits on the bad days when you're feeling down and uncreative. You'll open the book and say, "Look at that gift I gave my husband. Wow, I really spent time wrap-

ping that. I love the color of the paper, and where on earth did I find that ribbon? I'm going to use that color in my living room." Or maybe you'll open it up and remember how beautiful your tulips were last spring, and you'll notice how your garden style has changed since then.

A Style Scrapbook shouts, "Look at all the wonderful things I have created!" Once you begin to keep one, you'll be surprised at how many of your projects you actually photograph each day. Eventually, you won't even be able to keep up with your work. You'll be creating so much, you won't have time to run and get the camera. But, for now, keep a camera handy at all times and don't be shy with it.

table in a fabulous new way. Take a "before" shot of the table, then after you've pulled the whole thing together, take an "after" shot. Print them out and put them in your Style Scrapbook side by side as "before" and "after" pictures.

Start Styling
POP QUIZ

Now that you've gotten your feet wet and your hands dirty, put your styling smarts to the test—then move on to the next section.

1 **Name the five Senses of Style.**

2 **If a person describes something as "coarse," what style sense are they referring to?**

3 **What is a good solution for too many objects around the house?**

4 **True or false: A Style Diva should work by herself.**

5 **Describe the qualities of a Style Diva's attitude.**

6 **What's the purpose of acting like a child when creating?**

7 **What does it mean to give your home a new wardrobe?**

8 **When shopping for props, what are four important items to look for?**

9 **When I talk about your Away Style Team, to whom am I referring?**

10 **What are the two most important reasons for starting a Style Scrapbook?**

Get Inspired   Start Styling   Keep Creating   Get Inspired

Keep Creating

Circle
of Style

Keep Creating

I used to end every segment of *Surprise Gardener* with the line, "Keep creating—that's the joy of life." Why? Because to me, creativity is an ongoing process. It doesn't stop when you plant the final fern in your garden, and it's not over when you finally complete your dining room. There will always be new projects, new challenges, new rules to break, and new ways to push past everyone's expectations—including your own.

What's keeping you from showing your Style Divadom all the time? For most people, the issue is keeping the momentum up. They are stalled by challenges or let themselves get complacent. Not a Style Diva!

In this section, I'll help you visualize success and show you how believing in your abilities will get you through those really dark days when nothing seems to turn out right. I'll also give you my secrets for overcoming common style hurdles and how to break through creative blocks. You'll find out how to define that *personal style* of yours that's been growing more and more obvious with every styling choice you make. And finally, you will be able to write your own Declaration of Creative Independence just like our fabulous forefathers did!

Once you finish reading these secrets and put them into practice, go back to the beginning of this book and start all over again—that's what I do! Each time you start a new creation, you should start with Inspiration. This is all part of what I call the Circle of Style: Inspiration, Styling, Keep Creating. And you now have a round-trip ticket booked for the world of style with unlimited frequent flyer miles. May your travels always be filled with newness, adventure, and the pure joy of creating. Keep it up!

the diva wears pajamas

Don't put your creativity on the clock. It may not want to work regular nine-to-five hours. **A Style Diva doesn't always plan a time to start creating—it just happens.** While booking time with yourself during the day is a great habit and ensures you can mark something off your to-do list, ideas tend not to follow such an orderly schedule. So if that inspiration hits at odd hours, when the rest of the world is asleep, get up and act on it!

Sometimes when I can't sleep, I will get out of bed and go downstairs to my office, even in my pajamas, and work on a creative project. I love the quiet and peace of these times, when everyone in my household is cozy in their beds. It's actually when I feel the most inspired. I have written all of my books at night when the phone doesn't ring, e-mails have stopped, and the kids don't require my attention. Without all those distractions, my head is clearer and my focus sharper. I can get more done in three hours at night than eight hours during the day.

One holiday, I styled an entire room between the hours of 5:00 and 8:00 am. Try doing that during the day when the kids are running in every three minutes asking for snacks, your friends are calling to recruit you for a fundraiser, and there's dinner to get on the table. No way!

Am I tired after I pull an all-nighter or rouse myself up at the crack of dawn? Sure, sometimes. But the exhilaration I feel when I create just pushes me through any feelings of fatigue. As long as my eyes aren't closing and I can still think, I'm fine. Also, I find that when my mind is relaxed and my thoughts are still, I experience a greater freedom to create than I do during the day, when I'm pulled in all directions. **Sometimes being tired opens me up to terrific new ideas.** Try it and you'll see that it's best if you have no energy to fight off your Style Diva instincts. Being in a room at an unusual time of day, for instance, makes me see the whole room a different way. It's at these times that surprising ideas often come to me.

The key to using this time is to get straight to work. **Ideas, like dreams, tend to fade quickly if they're not captured immediately.** For instance, if you wake up and suddenly know exactly how to rework your bedroom, then get up and do it. Don't worry about what you're wearing. Changing into "work clothes" is just going to disrupt your train of thought. I have been known to be so caught up in what I was doing that I stayed in my pajamas and bathrobe until eleven in the morning. Now that's a secret I'm not sure I should share!

For those of you who are just not night owls, I suggest you go to sleep early so you can wake up early. Those quiet dawn hours are just as useful and inspiring as the night. (Again, watch the light—it's great at this time of day!) This way, you will get some quality styling time before you have to hit the day running. **Imagine how Diva-esque it would be to arrive at work and tell them that you planted six pots on your patio before coming in that morning!**

Style Divas can find inspiration even in the middle of their beauty sleep!

Diva DRILL: Dress for Success

Are your current pajamas ready to get up and work when you are? While there's a lot to be said for ones that are nicely worn, even slightly tattered, they still have to do justice to your Style Diva sensibilities. (Silk negligees just don't lend themselves to hanging boughs of evergreens at five in the morning.) If you'd be embarrassed to be caught doing anything but sleeping in your current nightwear, it's time to hit the stores for some "work clothes"—a great comfy set of pajamas that affords you freedom of movement and yet makes you feel creative just wearing them. (While you're at it, consider doing something about your slippers as well.)

At home, prep your bedside table for nightime inspirations, and be sure your Style Journal and a pen are close at hand so that when you wake up with an idea, you can get it down immediately and go back to sleep. (Those ideas will keep you up if you don't get them out of your brain right away.)

Finally, for those nights when you get up to work on a project, be sure you have something to fuel you. I love honey and lemon in hot water when I get up, or peach or peppermint herbal tea. I'll often toast a piece of whole grain honey bread with a little butter and fresh preserves.

don't follow trends-set them!

Style is never static. It is constantly moving in a definite direction. That direction is called a trend. You see trends in fashion. In the seventies, bell bottom pants were the rage. The eighties were all about big hair and shoulder pads, the nineties ushered in the "eco look" with white linen and thick cotton, and in the first decade of the twenty-first century, we've revived all these looks but put a new spin on them.

Home decorating trends have also changed. The decade of the seventies was a big time for shag carpets; the eighties brought us neon, high-energy colors; the nineties were about neutral colors, organic fabrics, and rough textured carpets like berber and sisal. Today, the geometric shapes that marked the mid-century modern style have returned, but they're being reinterpreted and used in a contemporary way. Interestingly enough, home trends often follow those in fashion. Each year trends change, and a Style Diva is always up on where they are going. She knows that if her space doesn't evolve,

even just slightly, with the times, in a very short while, the room will have gone from daring to dated.

Wait a minute, you're saying, I just finished this room and got it "just right." And now you're telling me I have to change it again? Well, yes. Even if you favor traditional styles, there's always an update that can be done or a way to refresh a room on its way to stagnation. Look for different colors and different textures that align with overall home décor trends. It's the difference between living in a home and living in a museum. For those who have spent fortunes on hiring decorators, this may not be music to your ears. Even for you, there are ways you can continue to create—and you should!

Being up on the trends doesn't mean a Style Diva is a trend victim— always changing her clothes, her home, her garden, just to be cool and current. It just means she likes to keep things fresh. Some trends she's going to love; others, well, she's happy to leave them. **A Style Diva knows that trends are ultimately made to be broken, and**

meanwhile she interprets them through her own personal style. But in order to put your own personal twist on a trend, you need to know what those trends are first. A true trendsetter knows every blip in the world of style, whether in fashion, home, or garden. Then she does what she wants anyway!

I've met some pretty daring trendsetters in my life, but I think the trophy has to go to Cher. I learned a lot watching her. She was family... like a sister-in-law. Cher is a trendsetter, always looking to be unique, to find something differ-ent, and to push the envelope. Whether she and Sonny were wearing bobcat vests or she was showing her navel on national television, she has always lived her life on her own terms, regardless of what

anyone else might think. She'll dress in some wild outfit by Bob Mackie at the Academy Awards if she feels like it or star in an off-beat movie (for which she then wins an Academy Award, of course).

139

And by pursuing this ongoing creative approach to life, she has stood out, been successful, and been the one to set many a trend. She doesn't let people deter her from her vision, and she is not afraid to follow her instincts. If anything, she actively looks to be different from everyone else—which is why she has such a distinctive sense of style. **If you are like everyone else, you just blend in. What makes you unique, different, special?**

A great example of Cher's approach to life and her ability to set trends (other than fashion) is the time she bought a plot of land in a rustic part of Benedict Canyon in Los Angeles near where Sonny and I lived after we sold the Bel Air house. This was by no means prime real estate. The property was pretty run down and dilapidated, the kind of dusty, arid spot that always seems to attract rattlesnakes and tumbleweeds. Even its wilting "For Sale" sign was covered with weeds. Oh, so perfect for a woman known for her sequin television-show outfits, right? Cher had a vision: She was going to

transform this bare lot into a spectacular Egyptian mausoleum. At the time, ancient Egyptian art and style were popular (King Tut was making his way around the country), but no one I knew was building homes in that style! I think a few of the neighbors thought she was nuts, but Sonny and I knew better. There are no rules in Cher's book.

Years later, the run-down plot became home to a magnificent Egyptian estate with grand gates and a spectacular drive. It was a huge, two-story house with exceedingly high ceilings. All the lines were very clean on the outside, yet the inside was filled with lots of softer exotic elements and wonderful textures. I especially loved the wonderful array of nubby, fuzzy, and textured fabrics and materials used. It was a very fun mix of unique elements that all came together in typical Cher style. That arid, rattlesnake-laden section of Benedict Canyon is now one of the most exclusive neighborhoods in Los Angeles. Of course, Cher has moved on to a new creative endeavor. **You can't keep a Diva down.**

A Style Diva is always one step ahead unless she feels like going retro.

Diva DRILL : Be a Trend Spotter

Go through a few fashion magazines and compile a list of five of the latest trends. Pay close attention to the styles, colors, textures, and silhouettes. Do the same thing with home décor catalogs or magazines. Write down five new trends, including colors, shapes, and styles. Now, take it to next level: How could you use them in your own home? Which one can you put a twist on? What happens if you take a current color and use a different shape with it and where does that lead? (And then, watch who starts to follow you!)

thinking outside the box

This has become a popular phrase among corporate executives and management consultants to motivate employees to think creatively. The idea is that if you are thinking outside the box, you are not confined by its boundaries. There are no limitations, no restrictions; everything is outside the norm. My question is this: Why would someone ever contain her ideas in the first place? **A true Style Diva tries to stretch as far out of the box as she can (then she uses the box as a decorative accessory!).** So how do you do this, too?

You start inside the box with normal, "safe" ideas. Then you allow your imagination to go a bit further out—further and further until you get to the point where you can look at a project broadly and in an unlimited fashion. The operative word to remember here is creating. You haven't *just* created, you're not *going* to create. You're

Diva DRILL : Shake It Up

Sometimes doing small things in a different way in your everyday life can help you get used to the idea of expanding your vision. All sorts of great and unexpected things can happen just by making subtle adjustments to your normal routine. You begin to see things differently, and you open yourself up to new experiences. I don't mean you should go to Tahiti unannounced in the middle of your workweek; I mean rent a movie you wouldn't normally see or go out when you usually stay in.

Now, write your most "out" ideas (outrageous, outlandish, outstanding) in your Style Journal, or choose a time to sit with your styling buddy and toss ideas back and forth. What can you do that is different and out of the ordinary? Do you always wear the same "no-fail"

creating all the time.

I took this approach with another book that I'm writing. It's a wedding style book. When I discussed this with my publisher, I made it known that I only wanted to do books that were "outside the box." So, my publisher hooked me up with a creative design firm that could help us put my vision together. They further broadened the scope of the project: the book is no longer just a lovely coffee-table book with pages and photos but is an entire interactive experience with accordian pullouts, inserted booklets, die-cut pages, gatefolds, and vellum sheets. We kept expanding on the idea until it wasn't just a book but an entire universe of wedding style inspiration for the reader. **What box are you ready to burst out of?**

outfit every time you hit the town? Do you shop at the same stores? Where will you go on your next vacation? The goal is to start small but dream big.

Apply this same practice to the world of style. If you always decorate in the same way—using the same colors and sensibilities—mix it up a little. Replace that monochromatic pillow with a pattern, or use velvet instead of linen. Have you used the same holiday table layout for a decade? If you always plan sit-down dinners, then plan a buffet or vice versa. Style Divas know that the creative process is never rigid, and a willingness to try new things is a big step towards realizing creations you never thought possible.

put aside perfection

I want to let you in on a little piece of wisdom that might take a load off your mind: In style, perfection is not your goal, and even the idea of it can stop you from wanting to create. What is perfection, anyway? One dictionary definition: "Being without defect or blemish [such as] a perfect specimen." That's a pretty tall order for an outdoor deck or living room! Don't even go there.

When some people get styling and begin to get things done, there comes a point when they feel they have to keep everything "just so." I put so much work into it, I'm sure not letting it get messed up again. But then your teenage son's size-thirteen athletic shoes are in the middle of the floor, or there's a stack of library books and scrapbooking material plunked down on the coffee table, or your six-year-old has gone and rearranged your prized collection of Zuni pottery. Yes, all great homes require a little maintenance. But that doesn't mean that yours has to be perfect all the time. Life goes on!

Momentary messes and unintentional placements can help trigger fresh inspirations for a room you thought was "done." When you stopped to pick up the shoes on the floor, you may have gotten a different view of your coffee table, one that made you think how it would look better on the other side of the room. The library books might have ended up on the table because there was a hole waiting to be filled by a deliberately placed vignette. And as for the six-year-old and the pottery—you know how I feel about the way kids see things!

On my daughter Hailey's most recent birthday, we had a tea party for her and her girlfriends. There were sofa cushions, dress-up clothes, and my old hats scattered everywhere! And wouldn't you know that all those lovely little girls were jumping on the sofa! So much for perfection at Chez Style Diva.

If you're single, live alone, never entertain, and basically don't do anything

in your home but sleep, then you might be able to maintain some sense of perfection. But then why would you want to live like that? That's a Style Diva drag! And don't be fooled by how perfect rooms look in home décor magazines. A team of professionals sweeps through the place and tweaks and tweaks for hours just to get a flower or throw to look right. If you had a team like that, I'm sure your place would look fabulous all of the time, too!

Don't think you have to hold yourself to the perfectionist ideal of getting one thing completely done before you begin another. Working on one thing at a time just doesn't work for me. I'll start in one room,

and it will inspire me to move something to another room, and then I'll start on that room then go back to the other. I go back and forth if necessary until I'm finished. I don't allow myself to be stuck trying to make things perfect, and I never stop creating. By styling more than one area at a time, I have time to try some ideas one place, move to another place, and then come back to view my first attempts with a fresh eye. This keeps the energy and the creativity flowing.

Ironically, I find that by moving around so much, I can get my work done much faster and burn calories at the same time! Multitasking is always good because most Style Divas don't have a lot of time on their hands.

Diva
DRILL : Deconstruction, Reconstruction

Find a display or arrangement that you feel is really great, the one you look at and think that it came out just right. Now take it apart. Challenge yourself to rethink every object you've included in it. Why are you still using it? Does it still speak to your mood, the season, current trends? Pare it down, add some new objects—even move its placement in the room—and work it into a fresh new statement. Does changing that particular display have a cascade effect, asking other things in the space to change as well?

every no gets you closer to yes

As you've no doubt figured out already, style is never just a walk in the park. There are always opposing obstacles, highs and lows, disappointments and doubts. That's what makes it so exciting! One frequent refrain I hear from people stuck in a rut is, "I just can't figure out what I like!" As I've shown you earlier in this book, the problem is rarely coming up with style ideas that you like. If you really think about it, you have strong opinions about your taste and sensibilities. The problem is sorting out the best of your ideas from the rest of your ideas.

Believe me, when it comes to style, you probably know more than you let on. You just have a problem choosing from all those options: What color should you paint the wall? What fabric is best for the sofa? What dishes should you buy for your more formal entertaining?

Here's a secret that works well for

Diva DRILL : Duck, Duck, Goose!

You know by now that a small change can have a big impact on a room. So head out to find a new set of accents for a room you're bored with, such as bath towels, candles, sofa pillows. There are bound to be many choices in the store.

You may have a good idea of what color you want, but there are so many varieties of that color that you don't know which one to choose. Pull the items off the shelves or display racks and line your choices next to each other. Now, eliminate your least favorite one by one, until you're left with a single item.

Or perhaps you're trying to coordinate towels with the new paint in the bathroom, and you want the towels to be the accent color. Go to

me and is bound to work for you, too. Ask not what you do like, ask what you don't like. By figuring out what doesn't work, you bring yourself closer to what does. When a Style Diva is overwhelmed with choices, she plays the elimination game. For example, if I'm looking for a particular green, I will pull ten shades and lay them out on the studio table. Then, one by one, I'll begin to cross colors off the list. "There's too much yellow in that green," I'll say, or "That one is too olive; that one is too evergreen; that one is too lime green."

I eliminate, eliminate, eliminate until I have narrowed it down to the final three. At that point it's usually pretty easy to choose one. But, as I have pointed out, it takes many no's before you can get to yes!

the paint store and pick up a variety of paint chips in the appropriate color palette. Rather than choosing the one you like first, choose the one you like least. Then choose your second least favorite color and your third until you narrow it down to the cream of the crop. Then go buy towels in that color!

the twenty-four-hour holding pattern

Sometimes you will finish something—a room makeover, a table setting, even a haircut—and just hate it, feel crummy, and think you are a Style Diva dunce. **Well, I always say before you get too upset with yourself, live with the change for twenty-four hours and then revisit it to see how you feel.**

For instance, my son, Hutton, recently needed a haircut. It had gotten quite long and although it actually looked fantastic, his school had a

rule about long hair. It took me over a month to convince him to get it cut. He always found some excuse. (You think teenage girls are obsessive about their hair? They've got nothing on the boys.) Finally we went to the salon together. As I watched the stylist snip away, I grew more and more nervous until I was sick to my stomach. It looked terrible. We both knew it. How would I talk to him? What could I say?

He wouldn't even speak to me on the way home, and when he finally did, he told me how he was never listening to me again and that I had ruined his life. I had been the one who assured him that this would be a very cool cut— even took him all the way to Hollywood to get it done by this fabulous hairstylist. Some good that did. There was nothing I could do except apologize.

The next day, he jumped in the shower and washed his hair. Maybe he hoped that if he watered it, it would grow back. I didn't dare say a word. He wandered into my bathroom looking for gel, molding mud, spray, anything that he could use to handle this hairy situation. He started working it and changing it. The next thing I knew he came out saying he actually liked it. I was shocked—it looked great!

We were not alone in our appreciation. He came back from school that day with a big smile on his face and told me that several people had remarked how cool his new hairstyle was. He thanked me and told me I was the world's coolest mom! So why did Hutton have such a big change of heart? He slept on it—literally and figuratively. Twenty-four hours gave him time to recharge and rethink his approach (from "nothing's ever going to make this look good" to "there's got to be something I can do") and to clear his head enough to make the style work for him.

So don't get too worked up if a styling project doesn't seem to be at its best. Sometimes you don't know right away what to do to change it. Or it may be that you've made a big change and you need time to adjust to it. Just sleep on it and get a fresh perspective in the morning. I do this all the time. A good night's sleep does wonders (who knows—you might get a middle-of-the-night, Diva-in-her-pajamas inspiration!) **If you still hate it twenty-four hours later, then do something about it.**

Diva DRILL : Dare to Be Different

Style a space completely different than you normally would. To help you focus on what to do differently, choose one Sense of Style to alter. Arrange a shelf extremely sparsely if you tend to do a lot of displays; put out rough-textured objects if you tend toward the smooth, and set hot-pink flowers into a container if you usually use cool blues or whites. Change it drastically!

It probably feels uncomfortable to you—it's so different from what you are used to. Now, give yourself a day with it. Come back and assess. Does it still look different, but good different? Or does it still feel completely out of kilter to you? Analyze which tweaks you can make, without redoing the whole thing, to bring it more in line with your sensibility.

time to play

Don't take style so seriously! I know it can be frustrating. I'm aware that it can be maddening. I realize it can be totally overwhelming. You're preaching to the choir. At any given moment I might have a product design, a proposal, and a television makeover due in the same week. So how does a Style Diva manage when she's in the midst of a category five style-storm? She gets playful. You have to switch gears and take it all in stride. **The tougher it gets, the more lighthearted you have to be. When I feel rigidity coming on, I approach creativity with a sense of play.**

I must say, I hit these moments frequently, and as you keep creating, so will you. When you are constantly creating, things are always expanding, which is the way you want it to be. A few weeks ago, we hit a category six style-storm where all things were due at once! We were all getting worn out, working late nights and tired in the morning.

As a result, we were a bit cranky, so one afternoon when I just had enough, I blasted the music in the office, and we all got up and danced. Hey, we even learned a few new moves! Although there are important issues and clients at stake, sometimes you just need a little break. **A sense of humor and a willingness not to take yourself or your projects too seriously are critical to your success.**

What I'm talking about here is freeing up your attitude. This sense of play affects every creative thing you do—from styling a room, to throwing a party, to even creating a big presentation at work. If you get so wrapped up in what can go wrong, what other people will think, how little time you have—well, you're going to close yourself off to all your best ideas. When this happens, Style Divas know the best solution is to have some fun and to approach creativity with a whole new viewpoint that says, **"I'm going to create. I'm going to be open. I'm not going to worry about anything for now. I'm just going to push past my limits, and, with a Diva as my witness, I'm going to enjoy doing it!"**

Diva
DRILL : Play Around

When you're fried, worried a project is not working, or just plain stuck, get away from what you're doing and set your sights on something else that is fun and creative. If you're out looking for new carpet and can't settle on one, go shopping for a new dress. Or go visit the garden store. Call your best friend and meet her for coffee. Or if you're agonizing about where to put the television, just put it in the most ridiculous place you can for a day so that new space might come to mind. Ready to weep because the Thanksgiving turkey is just not cooking and you've got fifteen hungry people in the living room? Get everyone to find what they can around the house for an instant Pilgrim-and-Indians dress-up game (yes, even the grownups). You'll soon be laughing so hard that you'll forget about the turkey (at least until it's finally done). The point is to find a way to break free, even be a little silly, and not take it all too seriously.

it *will* get done

Now that you've started styling and are well into your creative process, you're probably quite familiar with the nagging feeling of wanting to quit because it's just too hard or it's taking too long or you just don't have the time to get it right. But a Style Diva is always pushing forward and overcoming obstacles. She doesn't consider the notion that a project might not be completed. She's convinced it will get done.

Sure, there will be rough patches and trying moments when you will want to wave your ivory lace flag (Divas don't use plain white, even in surrender), but look at these "problems" more as walls to be scaled rather than roadblocks that prevent all forward motion.

This is a powerful attitude and brings with it a tremendous amount of energy and confidence. **Once you decide in your heart that something will get done, there's nothing that will stop you.**

I have to approach everything in my life with this mindset—otherwise I'd never be able to accomplish everything I do. At any given moment, I may be writing a book, doing a radio show, designing a luggage line—all simultaneously. **The secret to my success—and my sanity—is knowing that all these projects will get done as long as I am willing to push through and do what it takes.**

I remember one time when a last-minute meeting was called by a big company we worked with. We found out about it the day before, and I had to quickly prepare my presentation for six of the company's top executives. I wanted to have a completed proposal. The idea of walking in there empty handed was not an option. Sometimes you only get one shot, and it's important to let companies know how dedicated you are. It's a matter of integrity and wanting to do your best.

So we dropped everything and started on a proposal, and by 9:00 pm it was close to being done. The only thing left to do was go down to the twenty-four-hour copy shop to print the proposal on high quality paper.

Three of us headed down to the shop. The plan was to get the job done in an hour using three machines at once. Then we could get to bed before midnight and awake refreshed for the 10:00 am meeting.

When we arrived, we found two machines were broken and the other operating at half speed! At 3:00 am, two of us were still there, bleary-eyed and printing away. By 4:00 am, we were finally done, which gave us barely enough time to catch a few hours sleep and grab a shower before heading out. I felt like we'd been up all night cramming for a test! But it had to be finished no matter what, and we just decided there was no other choice. We couldn't reschedule, call in sick, or stall for time. We were going to be at that meeting with a full proposal.

In the end, it paid off. The meeting was a big success! Even though there are problems to face and barriers to overcome, the drive to finish creates energy and momentum that always propels everything forward. Yes, we were all exhausted for that meeting, but we pulled it off. The feeling of accomplishment and pride was worth getting only two hours of sleep. **When you push through barriers in your life no matter how big or small, you will get rewards that you never dreamed possible. I assure you!**

Diva DRILL: Get It Finished

The next time you have the urge to put down a project for a while, try to recognize whether you're at risk of never completing that project. Is it something you've been putting off? Something you never seem to have time for? Instead of procrastinating again, keep working on it until you're completely done and completely satisfied with it. Skip lunch or dinner if necessary. Stay up into the wee hours—just keep going until you've pushed yourself through to the end. You'll feel a huge sense of relief that comes with freeing yourself of that responsibility and leaving room for something new. I don't recommend you handle all projects this way, but sometimes our unfinished business can follow us, slowing us down. Don't let snags, creative blocks, or exhaustion stand in your way. Remember, you are a Diva!

give yourself a deadline

While you shouldn't put a timeline on your creative hours, you can benefit from giving yourself a deadline every now and then. I know, I know—this is not a Style Diva's favorite concept. If she had her druthers, she would create concepts for all eternity. That's her nature—boundless ideas and enthusiasm. But, she also realizes that sometimes the world demands things get done in a timely manner. **A Style Diva is a dreamer, but she's also a realist.** I face strict deadlines in my work all the time.

I was once asked by *The View* to do a segment on making over the "World's Ugliest Bedroom." They found one in Boston, where two twenty-something sisters shared a tiny, narrow bedroom that was crammed with two large mismatched beds and two mismatched chests of drawers. They had clothes strewn everywhere and laundry baskets in the middle of the floor. There was barely any room to breathe. Plus, on the walls there were two different kinds of old wallpaper—stripes and floral—making the space even less appealing.

We had two weeks to prepare and only one day to do the actual makeover. This was a tall order considering: a) we could not see the location in person so we worked off of a homemade videotape and a few dimensions; b) we had to order headboards and mattresses and coordinate the delivery and receipt from Los Angeles; and c) we had to do

Diva DRILL : Manic Makeover

Give yourself one hour to redo a room, maybe for an upcoming holiday or change of season. Set aside the hour at a time when you simply must be out of the house in sixty minutes. For instance, you have to pick up kids, meet people for dinner, get to a doctor's appointment. Pull out whatever you have at hand and just go, go, go.

What happens when you don't have time to second guess yourself?

the final prop shopping the evening before the makeover in Boston, and we didn't know the town.

We used bedding from my collections, so that was the easiest part, but the rest of the products had to be found. Since they were young we chose a fun lime-green paint to contrast against one of my bedding collections, which was a black and taupe.

When we finally arrived in Boston, we faced problem after problem. First, the paint was totally the wrong shade. Solution: we ran to the paint store, got another shade, and mixed it right there on the spot. Second, the painters arrived later than expected, and at one point we weren't sure they were showing up at all! Solution: we spackled and painted over the wallpaper, which requires priming and drying and three coats just to cover it.

We almost didn't make it to the finish line before dark, but in the end everything was completed. **Deadlines do that. They limit your choices, fine-tune your focus, and help you gain confidence in your styling solutions.** We styled the room, transforming it from "the ugliest bedroom in America" to the most beautiful.

The girls loved their new bedroom so much that they sat on their beds and cried with joy. They had lost their mother a few years back, and their home needed a woman's touch. I was proud to be their mom for the day. This meant so much to them, and they were very thankful. **The deadline might have been tight, but the rewards were far-reaching and outweighed any struggles.**

How do you feel when you're done? What decisions were you able to make on the fly? How did the room look when you were done? If you feel the room is still not quite right, then give yourself another hour when you can in order to finish up. I want you to be happy with the results, but the goal is to get it done! You're working that style muscle again, and over time this exercise will make you stronger and faster.

embrace chaos

You know the scenario (or can imagine it): You have a grand vision for redoing your kitchen in a Tuscan style, complete with copper pot racks, wrought iron accents, and stone floors. You've found your materials and hired your contractors, but as the masons arrive to lay the floors, you realize the stones are the wrong color! Or the plumber discovers that he can't run the

BEFORE THE BEGINNING OF GREAT BRILLIANCE, THERE MUST BE CHAOS.

water line where you wanted it
to be for the new oversized farm
sink. He thinks they'll have to move it,
and you think you're just going to SCREAM.
Why can't anything go as planned?!

But plans are just plans—not reality.
And reality changes on the fly. The thought
of changing all the plans you've made so
far has frozen you in your tracks. Perfectly
understandable. Change in the middle of
a project can be scary. But fear is useless
when the situation is calling for you to be
creative. **As a Style Diva, you need to give
yourself permission to change and get
over your fear of making a mistake.**

As the I Ching, an ancient Chinese
source of proverbs, says, "Before the
beginning of great brilliance, there must be
chaos." And let me tell you, no professionally done creative endeavor—from writing
a novel to producing a fashion shoot—is
without chaos. Novelists, photographers,
magazine editors, directors, and actors all
hone their creativity through meeting on-
the-fly challenges.

It rains on the day when the script calls
for sun. The star model is stranded in Lux-
embourg due to a missed plane connection
from her last job. Palm trees show up when
the creative director specifically asked
for pine trees. Stuff happens. **It's how you
handle this stuff that separates the true
Divas from the wannabes.**

Sometimes chaos comes in the form of
new ideas entering the arena at the last minute. For instance, one of my girlfriends was
creating an outdoor room with a fireplace,
new tile, a seating area, a bar—the works. I
came over for dinner the night before her
contractor was to begin and gave her some
new suggestions after looking at her plans.
She had worked months to finalize these
plans, and now she felt she really should
make those changes. (That's what Style

and not to come the next day. She figured out how she could incorporate some new ideas—including a pizza oven—and is now thrilled that she stopped the process and switched gears.

Diva friends are for.) She had two options: either to get all stressed out, or to go with the new plans, even if it made all of the other plans go awry.

In true Style Diva form, she went with the chaos and called her contractor. She told him she was regrouping

Pay attention to the difference between stress and chaos. Chaos is life at work—new situations and new ideas arising as you work. Stress is not the definite end result to chaos, it's merely one possible reaction to it. The

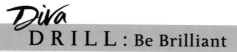

Diva DRILL: Be Brilliant

The next time chaos hits, look for the secret brilliance that is in its wake. Sit down with your Style Journal and confront the chaos head on. What in particular is making you feel off-balance? Is it that the paint doesn't match the stone floor? Is the entranceway to the kitchen not going to be done in time for a big dinner you have planned? Are there just too many people around? Now brainstorm ideas that would overcome the challenge brought on by chaos. Maybe it's a new shade of paint to better match the stone floors, a way to artfully drape fabric

other possible reaction is to act like a Diva and respond to the new ideas, find a way to make it happen despite deadlines, and go for the dream. **Work with what you've got, and make what you've got work. It's the Diva way.**

A Style Diva's ability to 'throw something together' can be compared to Michelangelo's ability to look at a slab of marble and 'knock something out.'

over the doorframe to hide the work in progress, or a better way to schedule the contractors. There's always an answer if you trust yourself and take a moment to let the ideas come.

stop apologizing

Everyone has her own unique creative process. And one is not better than the other. Some people are very systematic in their approach; some are very free and loose. Some people know exactly what they want. They go to the store, buy something, bring it back home, and know just where it's going to go. I personally prefer to look at something from many different viewpoints before making a final decision. I like a lot of options. For me, that's the part of the creative process that I love—finding a way to do something and then finding another way and then another way.

It's like a painter. She'll sit at her easel, drawing sketch after sketch, as a pile of crumpled up paper collects at her feet. She's looking at colors and strokes and lines—trying to find the perfect combination. Sometimes those discarded sketches become works of art in themselves because they capture the creative process.

Once you find your own creative process (and you probably have by now), you need to accept and embrace it as a part of who you are. Don't let anyone say, "You're taking too long," or "Can't you just make a decision and get on with it?" You know exactly how to create because you've done it before. You're doing it right now. Relish the process, not just the result. **Test your imagination and come up with interesting and provocative new ideas. Acknowledge them, try them, and be willing to change them if you come up with ones you like better.** That is the creative process, so don't you ever say you're sorry about it again.

Here's another tip: you'll find yourself apologizing a lot less if you surround yourself with those who cheer you, not jeer you. No one but you has the authority to judge your work—but that doesn't mean they won't try. You'll finish a project and invite people over to see it, and suddenly, *everyone is a critic.*

When someone tells you they don't like something you've created and it makes you feel awful, don't just take it to heart and suck it up. Although the intention probably wasn't to hurt you, those negative comments are detrimental to your creativity. It can be a major buzz kill, in fact. If you are a Shy Style Diva, it may have taken you a lot just to finish that one project that you were so proud of. Do not let anyone take that away from you. What you are really looking for is encouragement, and you should only listen to feedback from those who give constructive criticism—if they criticize at all.

Diva DRILL: Sorry Diary

In your Style Journal, write down five creative activities you have apologized for in the last month or year. These can include anything from changing your order three items at a restaurant to going "office casual" to a meeting with a very formally dressed client. Maybe you chose to use the "wrong" paint in your bathroom. Now, think about why you were apologizing. Is it because you weren't happy with the outcome, or is it because others were critiquing your process or choices (either implicitly or explicitly)?

Are you even apologizing for things you couldn't control? For instance, were you called into that meeting without warning? If there are things you could do better next time (for instance, keep a change of clothes and dress shoes in your office), note them. But if you're apologizing to make someone else feel better at your own expense, it's time for some self-affirmation: You are a Style Diva!

why isn't this working?

Take a look at your projects. Some have come out great. Congratulations! But there are one or two that you see that aren't quite right, and it bothers you every time you look at them. You don't love them.

I've explained how you can use the Five Senses of Style to decide what should go into creating a space or vignette. They're equally important for analyzing what shouldn't go in or what should come out. Take a good look at your creation. Now, ask yourself whether your style is consistent. Are all the elements aligned with the style you've picked? For example, have you put a funky bowl on the table of your Queen Anne-style dining room?

Pull out the offending object and see if things work better together. Okay, if that wasn't it, look at color. Do the individual colors align with the palette? Too many colors? Take something out.

The next things to consider are shape and proportion. Are the shapes too similar? Maybe you need to add a contrasting shape. Is that huge vase overwhelming the other accessories in your vignette? Or maybe the vase is too small for the end table you've put it on. Look for absences of shape or size, as well.

Take a buffet table, for instance. Have you used only round platters for serving? Add a few oval ones. Is everything just flat on the table? Set a tall

vase or several candlesticks at the end of the long buffet table to give it some height. Or perhaps placing some of the plates on pedestals or tiered racks will add some dimension. You can also use overturned bowls as risers under your tablecloth. I've even used kids' lunchboxes!

If all that's working, focus on the arrangement itself. Have you tried to group your items together tightly, but now they all look scrunched up? Space them out ever so slightly. Have you gone overboard with trying to keep things symmetrical so that everything is in twos, twos, and more twos? Perhaps you set out everything exactly evenly spaced—two round plates exactly six inches to either side of an oval one on a buffet. Change the space between them a bit. Keep playing until it feels good and appears balanced and harmonious to your eye.

There's no perfect way to lay out a table, vignette, or room—and don't let anyone ever tell you there is! Trust me, that is what style is all about. You have to consider both the elements in a space individually and the look of everything as a whole. Adding, removing, or moving one thing can change the balance one way or another. You have to just keep going until your inner Style Diva says it's right. **If you want to have your home reflect your own personal style then you can't follow rules—unless they are your own style rules.** You need to free yourself up to create something that is unique from everything and everyone else.

Diva DRILL : It Ain't Over Until the Style Lady Sings

There comes a time in the midst of any project when you ask yourself, Why doesn't this look like it should? What's wrong with me? Why can't I do anything right? Hel-loooo: Is this any way a Style Diva should talk? No— but yes. You should ask yourself what's not working when a room or space isn't turning out like it should, but you should not tear yourself apart over it. Tear apart the arrangement instead.

Listen to your inner Style Diva on this point. Take the time to identify

what's not working for you. Go through the five Style Senses. Analyze the lighting. Maybe it's a pillow that looked great at the store but doesn't work with what you've got at home. Maybe the paint color you chose is a touch off—that salmon pink is too orange in the daylight. When you've hit on what the issue is, rework it until it's right to you. Remove the thing that doesn't work. Repaint the room. Swap the flowers on the table for different ones. Just do whatever it takes to make your Style Diva sing with joy!

try, try again

Finding brilliance in chaos, letting go of perfection—that's all well and good, you say. But what about when it's a complete flop and there's no rescuing it? Sadly, into every Diva's life a little failure must fall. But after you've cried into your pillows, it's time to dust yourself off and put your stylish best back on.

The fact is, style victories come out of trial and error. If you let yourself be defeated by one setback or convince yourself you are a failure because you didn't get it right the first time, you'll lose your nerve to try anything new. Before you start doggedly down the same path, though, assess why it didn't work the first time. Perhaps you used the wrong techniques or maybe you chose the wrong materials or there was some other flaw in your plan. **The key is to identify what didn't work before you go at it again.**

For instance, let's say you put in a shade garden last year and you've been looking forward to those bleeding hearts, primroses, and lilies of the valley all winter. But here it is spring, and you've got a barren little plot. Nothing came up. Did you think that space, since it was shady, was also moist? Go check it. Maybe it's actually pretty dry since a large maple is near it and sucks up all the moisture. Before you replant in the same spot, find out how you can amend the soil, change watering patterns, or even choose different plants. Perhaps a container garden would work better here, at least for the season, so you can cover up the bare patch. There is always an answer and many resources for advice.

Or maybe, after hours of agonizing over a color choice, you realize something is not right. You don't have to live with it; it's okay to redo it. These are sometimes not inexpensive errors. I remember on two occasions when friends bought the wrong color wall-to-wall carpet and had to replace it. That kind of mistake can sting, but a Style Diva finds a way to get through it and comes out the wiser.

In the end, that's what you have to count as a triumph: the wisdom you gain from what went wrong. It's useful to keep track of your failed projects, whether it's a recipe, a table setting, or a garden. These failures are often just lessons waiting to be learned! Even though a Style Diva can accept that she can fail, she doesn't accept failure. It's not one of her Senses of Style.

Style Divas don't give up; they create ways to make things happen.

Diva DRILL : Face the Failure

Failures come in all sizes, just like victories. To get comfortable with the process of trial and error, begin with a small project that really didn't work, and really study it. In two columns in your journal, itemize what went wrong and what went right (there had to be something). Was it the materials? Maybe you were working on a mosaic flower pot, but you used a glue that wasn't waterproof, and when you set it out, it fell apart in the first rain. Did you not give yourself enough time, or did you skip a critical step? Did you let someone else pressure you into making a decision you weren't sure about? (Sure those hibiscus were on sale, but did you really want them?) Did you compromise on your vision? Now that you know what didn't work, do it over in a manner that will correct your mistakes but keeps what did work.

when the thrill is gone

Sometimes holding on to certain items traps you and limits your creativity. I'm not talking about the pieces that you have sent off to "retreat" or the sentimental goods you have on display. Those are special and have value to you. I'm referring to that pitcher you received as a wedding present that once was your favorite vase but is never used anymore or the painting you picked up at a garage sale that seemed like such a good purchase at the time but now looks totally out of place in your den. It's not that these items aren't nice, they've just lost their appeal. It's sort of like wearing the same sweater year after year. After a while, you get tired of it and need to move on. The magic has faded.

There's tremendous power in removing items that you have outgrown. **By creating a void, you make the space for new energy or items to come in.** It's not just the physical act of getting rid of the clutter, but it's also a mental release of the past. By opening up your space to new objects, you open up your experience to new ideas. Don't let the investment you made in a large piece hold you back, either. Think you paid too much for that furniture to ever justify getting rid of it, even though you're sick of it? Get creative with how you remove it. You don't have

Diva DRILL: Don't Live with What You Don't Love

Identify three pieces in your home that you're done with. If you never see them again, it'll be too soon. Now, bring them to a consignment shop, post them on eBay, or team up with your neighbors to have a block-long garage sale. (They probably have stuff they're ready to get rid of too!) Put the proceeds from the sale into your "re-styling" fund, and use it only to buy new pieces that speak to the style direction you're heading in now.

to leave it out on the curb!

For instance, I once had some wonderful patio furniture that had been given to me by friends years earlier when they had bought their new set. Now that I was done with the furniture and ready to move on, I decided I would take the pieces to a consignment shop. They were collectible mid-century modern pieces, after all! I called the shop, and the owner virtually jumped through the phone. He came immediately, picked them up, and paid me on the spot. It was enough to buy two new chaises, a loveseat, two chairs, a Morroccan mosaic table, and six dining chairs. **The void created a space for new furniture and some extra cash. Never a bad thing!**

As you can see, selling off old belongings does more than clear your space for new acquisitions—it can help fund them. You can also try trading pieces with friends (I do this all the time) in order to both dispose and acquire at the same time. **But don't stay married to an object once the passion has burned out. That's a sure way to live unhappily ever after.**

lock into a vision-and look out!

Anyone I know who has had great success in creative endeavors, or any successful endeavors for that matter, has a clear vision. Without it, you can get lost, distracted, and hung up on all those little issues that sidetrack you from your dreams. A vision is like a hot knife through butter—it cuts through the fat. When I talk about vision, I'm not referring to some New Age concept involving crystals and chanting. **Quite simply, vision is a clear goal that drives you forward, keeps you motivated, and gives you the passion needed to reach your goal.**

Once you have the vision, you need to practice seeing it clearly in all its multifaceted, technicolor brilliance. That's how I've always approached creativity. After all, the Diva is in the details. I believe that if I can truly see something in my mind, visualize every inch of it, in as much detail as possible, the vision will materialize.

I've seen it happen time and time again. One morning, I was scouting out locations for a photo shoot, and one of the places I saw was a beautiful home in Pasadena. The door opened, and I was greeted by a familiar face that I hadn't seen in years. He was a fashion stylist that I'd worked with when I was a model. He now had this incredible old Spanish estate that he'd redone. We recognized each other immediately. After we reminisced a bit, he invited me inside and gave me a tour of his home. The entire place was a model of good taste and eclectic, wonderful finds. His home even had a secret passageway behind the bookcase, which my Hailey and Hutton would have loved. Talk about a dream spot—a secret place to get away and breathe for a moment where no one could find me!

We continued upstairs and came to the guest room. I walked in and stopped dead in my tracks. There was the bed I had seen on the cover of a home decorating magazine over a year ago. When I first saw it, I felt so strongly about it that I tore the cover off the magazine and put it in my Style File. It was the very bed that I wanted

for Hailey's room. I'd imagined putting a princess canopy above it using one of my mother's saris. But it was an antique and impossible to find. I would look at it periodically when I went through my file for inspiration. I knew that little bed by heart!

There I stood in front of the exact bed, with my mouth open. I told my friend that I had seen a very similar bed in a magazine and how much I loved it. He then informed me that it was for sale. He made me a deal I couldn't refuse, and I bought it right there on the spot. It now sits in Hailey's room with the pink saris with silver embroidery draped over it. It's a bed for my little princess!

I never would have recognized the opportunity right in front of me if I had not had such a clear vision of what I wanted. **When you know what you want, opportunities have a way of presenting themselves.**

Diva DRILL : Story Board It

In your journal, describe your ideal vision of your home. Give the space a story. What kind of mood, what kind of events take place? Who is there with you? Let your imagination go, filling in details of the furniture, colors, and so on, that make that event come alive on the page. Now, take your story and create a style inspiration board around it. Add images from your Style File and objects or pictures that speak to your vision. This board is your Vision Board—the North Star you'll follow throughout your style quests.

live by your own rules

As you may have noticed by now, **I'm not a big fan of rules.** In fact, I never met a rule I didn't want to break. (I'm sort of an outlaw of the style set.) It's not so much that I dislike rules in principle—in fact, I think they can have some value in keeping you focused and setting up boundaries. **I just don't like other people's rules imposed on me.** Like all Style Divas, I'm more than happy to walk to the beat of my own drum, design and decorate to the rhythm of my own instincts, and live the way I want to live.

Ever since I was in high school, I've lived by my own rules—even if it might get me in trouble. By the time I reached my senior year, I already had all the credits I needed to graduate, so I opted to be part of the work/study program and go to school in the morning and work the rest of the day as a secretary. I had skills! I landed a job at the National Heart and Lung Institute in Bethesda, Maryland. Since there was no way I was dressing like a typical secretary—

no skirts below the knee or wire-rimmed glasses for me—I gave myself the challenge to set a new fashion trend for the government. I would become the new Secretary of Style. This was Washington, DC, after all. Hey, I was seventeen years old and could type seventy-five words a minute with dead-on accuracy, so I figured they wouldn't fire me!

People asked me where I got my confidence. I didn't know the answer. I just did what felt right, and often I got away with it. As much as I wanted to be like others and fit in—as most teenagers do—I also wanted to be an individual and make my own statement as well.

I had to stick to my guns and let the rules for my life trump everyone else's. Otherwise, I might have short-circuited my entire life—no modeling career, no acting, no restaurants, no stores, no HGTV, no Style Diva!! What a horrible thought!

Your signature style rules reveal themselves when you put everything you've worked on—your vision, your mission, your attributes—together in a consistent way and apply them to everything you do. It comes across in how you dress, how you entertain, how you style your home, even the attitude you take toward life. It's an overall approach to how you live your life and the statement you make in doing so. That is the essence of your signature style—your rules. It's all about making something uniquely yours, putting your flair on it. It's not about the label or what's in. **It's about how you do something, how you put it together. It's your personal statement, your unique way of doing things.**

Diva DRILL: What Are *Your* Style Rules?

Creating your own rules and living by them can sometimes bring up insecurities. You may have trouble seeing yourself as an independent thinker. I bet you think you don't have many of your own style rules. Think again! Sit down with your Style Journal and make a list of your own style rules that you've followed for you home. "I will only buy neutral colored sofas so that I can add color with decorative pillows and throws and change frequently." Or "I only like warm colors—no cool colors for me."

Now your list can—and should—go beyond the home. Think of some of your other rules you've used to style your life, such as, "Always write thank you notes; make my own cards; get to the gym three times a week to stay in shape; don't let the garden get unruly." I bet the rules you wrote down are the ones you're the least willing to break. You've been living on your own terms for some time. Reevaluate which ones work for you and throw out the rest!

communicate through your style

When you think of communication, what comes to mind? Talking to someone on the phone, writing letters, text messaging until your thumbs get tired? All of those things are valid.

Communication is simply the passing along of ideas and information. What it doesn't say (and what you may not have thought about right away) is that style is also a form of communication.

Style, specifically, your personal style, reflects how you view the world and how you want the world to view you. It's not just something you have or something you want. It's the way you express yourself and put your personal mark on everything you do.

Always remember that your style makes a statement. Whether you want it to or not, it is reflected in everything that you do. Take your home, for example. You can communicate so many different messages just by the way you put things together. Let's say someone walks into your living room and it's very neat and tidy. Not an object is out of place. It feels almost like a museum. This sends a definite message to the visitor: *You'd better take off your shoes before you walk inside; if you*

move a pillow, you'd better put it back in its place. To some, it might even sound like: *I value my stuff more than I do people; you have to do it my way.*

If you were to walk into another home with a more relaxed vibe, the message might be: It's fine to curl up on the couch and grab a pillow or sit down and stay for a while. "Let's talk" is what visitors are likely to hear. In both instances, the home also communicates something about the owner—how she lives her life, what's important to her, what her sense of style is. A home might not have a voice, but it speaks volumes.

The style of your home can also reflect your history, your passions, your interest. I've noted previously how I love to bring in plant material to style

my home. I'm passionate about land-scaping and gardening, and I love using florals everywhere I can, including my product designs. My Indian heritage has given me a deep appreciation of exotic colors and textures, which I use throughout my home and garden and with all things I style. And of course, I developed my love for Parisian style early on. The point is, if you look closely at my style, you can see my life and loves written into it quite clearly.

Style to me is an incredible mode of communication, one that everyone should take advantage of. It's not just about having a pretty home or impressing someone. It's about being proud of who you are, where you have come from, and what you do to live your life well. It's your personal statement of who you are and what you represent. By understanding and embracing this, you can expand all areas of your living. People will look at you differently, your place will be changed, you'll experience eating and restaurants in a new fashion, you'll shop differently. Most important of all, you will be proud of your accomplishments and will want to share them with others.

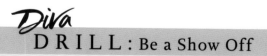

Diva DRILL : Be a Show Off

Who are you? Does your home reflect that image? Give yourself fifteen minutes to write down a list of adjectives in your Style Journal that best describe your personality, and don't worry if you come up with some (or many) synonyms. For instance, *dynamic, exotic, energetic, whimsical, sassy, on-the-fly, flexible, determined*. These are your personality and style attributes. Using these descriptions of yourself to help set your personal style direction is what will make your style your own. Now, look around your home. Is that reflected in your displays? Or

A Style Diva's style makes a statement —

it is reflected in everything she does.

have you made your home very formal because that's how you think it "should" be? Choose one space that you feel doesn't convey who you are and rework it to literally show yourself off.

the evolution of your style

As your Style Diva skills and confidence start to soar, you can begin combining styles and updating your place regularly. Does the idea of combining a rustic urn with a mod love seat freak you out? It shouldn't. You can introduce elements from different styles—if you do it with your eye on the Five Senses of Style—and have them live happily ever after in a harmonious marriage. This is how rooms and spaces stay fresh and current. I don't just mean in terms of trends (although that comes into play here). **You are constantly changing and evolving, and your space has to do that with you.**

These days, I live in a 1927 Spanish Bungalow. It has archways and painted wood, high-beam ceilings, and lots of French doors and windows. Mahogany wood trims the doors; the floors are a mixture of Spanish tile and wood. There's even a vintage stained glass window of a ship crossing the ocean! The base of my furnishings is exotic pieces from around the world. But I've added more contemporary pieces, as well. And of course, I'm always chang-ing around accessories.

So how do I keep the whole thing focused? Despite the differences in style references, there's a great deal of unity among them in the colors, textures, and shapes. The wood and tile of the house marry well with the rich tropical woods from which my exotic furniture is crafted. There's a simplicity and cleanliness to the lines of the archways and tile that allow for some contemporary pieces to work well in the space. And I use a neutral palette for the base of my furniture so I can add modern and more colorful accents with my accessories.

All this didn't happen overnight. I owned most of the furniture before I moved in, and each of those pieces has a history and was collected over many years. My piano, for example, came through an exchange with a friend who wanted my twig bed. I got the piano I wanted, she got the bed she wanted—a trade made in heaven! (Style Divas live for this sort of stuff.)

Luckily the piano is white and very contemporary. If I want to make it more exotic, I cover it with a tapestry or textured runner. For a more contemporary look, I uncover it and place simple architectural vases on top and add a large flower arrangement. **Many of my other pieces can morph from one style to another because they are pretty neutral.** My sofas are a neutral linen color, and they have been used with every color palette and style I can think of. All it took was some throws and pillows. Thank goodness for soft goods!

Diva DRILL: Oh, Grow Up!

What space in your house has been "as is" for too long? Look for a room or area that you styled a few months, or even years ago. Perhaps it's a child's room. Your charming baby girl is now a pre-teen begging for a style update now. You're probably not going to get rid of all the furniture, and there are certainly mementos both you and she want to keep. But she's growing up, and you need to do something to satisfy her more mature tastes.

Begin by defining the style you have. Perhaps you had her room very charming and frilly when she was young. What colors, shapes, and textures did you use—a lot of eyelet lace, pink coverlets and accessories, white furniture with romantic curves? Now think (and perhaps discuss with her) where it can go from here. Maybe she still wants it "girly" but not so "babyish." Begin with the colors. If you go from baby-girl pink to a muted rose-pink or a rich fuschia in the bedcoverings and so on, will that help? If you replace the eyelet frilled curtains with a gauzy, plainer window covering, will that lend the sweet romantic feel you've got going everywhere else in the room but in a more modern way in deference to her sensibilities?

Perhaps you can distress the furniture or even replace her headboard to be a bit more rustic-romantic. And of course—do a full clutter-removal on her knickknacks and mementos! She will probably enjoy creating shadow-box displays of her favorite things with you. Next thing you know, you've not only updated the room—you've helped her Style Diva start to shine!

share your gift with others

Over the last ten years, I have been styling makeovers for television shows. In fact, even before I was doing it professionally, **I was the Makeover Queen, helping friends anytime they asked.** Talk about free labor! They would just call me over for lunch or dinner, and the next thing I knew, I was moving furniture and revamping the room. Don't get me wrong. I loved doing makeovers, but no one ever really returned the favor. No one had ever done a makeover for me.

Cut to Christmas a few years ago. I'd just bought a second home in Palm Desert, and I planned on spending the day after Christmas there with my kids. I had warned them not to expect much this year, since we had just moved a few months before and we didn't have

a lot of holiday decorations at that house. We took a few things with us anyway just to make it a little festive.

It was only a two-hour drive, and we arrived around eight that night. Hutton, my fifteen-year-old, took the key and went to open the front door. As he walked inside, he turned back to me and said, "Mom, you left the television on."

"No, I didn't," I replied

"Yes, you did."

"That's impossible—I haven't been here in weeks. Maybe Chris (a friend who had stayed there for the last few days) forgot to turn it off?" As I spoke, I realized that didn't make sense because Chris is meticulous and not the kind of person who would do such a thing.

A little nervous, I opened the door slowly. Soon I realized it wasn't the television but Christmas music playing from the stereo. Well, that didn't make sense either, as I didn't have a stereo yet. As we all peered inside to see if it was okay, we were astonished to see a beautiful topiary evergreen tree with lights and stars shining bright, sitting atop a table at the end of the living room; three stockings hanging over the fireplace and stuffed to the brim; a garland of twinkling lights strung on the fireplace; candles; greenery and more. Beyond the living room, just past the sliding glass doors that led out to the patio, there stood a blow-up snowman smiling at us in a whimsical fashion. I had thought these blow-ups (a big trend that year) were tacky when I first saw them, but now I was in love with mine! Such whimsy and fun!

My eyes started to well up with tears. Looking over at Hutton and Hailey, who were awestruck, I said. "Brian did this."

Hutton nodded and said, "Mom, what a good friend." My dear friend and styling buddy, Brian, knew that I had been working and traveling like crazy all the way up to the holiday, and he knew that I wouldn't have time to decorate my new home in the desert.

We moved on to the kitchen—tears of joy pouring down my cheeks—and saw a Santa cookie jar filled with cookies. There were also two red dishtowels, and chocolates in the refrigerator. In the kids' bedroom, we discovered two felt reindeer heads (each on a stick so you could play with it) peeking out above the bed pillows. At the end of their two beds were big fuzzy reindeer slippers with bells on them.

In my bedroom, there were reindeer slippers for me, too, and I put them on right away, as the kids had done with theirs. I just sat on the bed and cried soft tears. This had been a tough Christmas—the first one I'd spent single in fourteen years. This was Brian's gift to me, and the joy it brought is something I will never forget as long as I live.

I am not used to having someone give my home a makeover, or letting them do anything for me for that matter. I am very independent and used to doing things by myself. After nine years of surprising homeowners, I was now being given a great gift...it was now my turn to be surprised.

182

Diva DRILL : Surprise a Friend

Style Divas—you have such incredible talents to share. If you ever have a chance to do this for a friend or loved one, it is an amazing gift. It's not important how much you spend—there's no price you can put on the effort and caring it takes. If you have a mother, father, wife, or friend who loves the garden, you can give the garden a makeover, plant fresh annuals, or redo the living room with some fresh new pillows. If it's for Dad, clean out his tool shed and buy him organizers and such. Or how about freshening up a bedroom with a new bedding set? Or new towels and accessories for the bathroom? You should have even more styling skills after reading this book, so go all out! That kind of love goes a long way, and it's something that will never be forgotten.

let freedom reign

Ask yourself this question: **What would style be like if you removed fear and worry from the equation.** Pretty fun? Pretty free? The best way to overcome this fear is to do, do, do. When it comes right down to it—what are you really afraid of anyway? Maybe it's the unknown. Maybe you're concerned about investing all this time and energy into something that might turn out crummy, something that you might not feel proud of, or something that might make

you feel like you've failed. All these mights don't make it right. In moments like these, you need to call on your inner Style Diva to guide you.

I love to feel free, everyone does. And to be truly creative, you have to act free, think free, be free—and the only one who can liberate you is you. "How can I be free," you think, "when I have all these responsibilities, all these must-do's, all these restrictions on my time and finances?" Freedom is a mindset, and it enables you to take risks. It lets you say yes to the un-

Style Divas aren't afraid to take risks.

known—and no to unnecessary conventions. If you want to get up and running, you've got to pen your own Declaration of Creative Independence and live by it!

When our Founding Fathers set down to write the Declaration of Independence, they had no real idea of what they'd gotten themselves into. Live without a king? How unheard of! But they did it anyway, and from one simple document, they began to create an entirely new nation that would be run an entirely new way. And actually, with a few minor changes, it works great for a Style Diva, too:

We hold these truths to be self-evident: that all Style Divas are created equal, that they are endowed by their Creator with certain unalienable Rights: that among these are Life, Liberty and the pursuit of Happiness...

Whenever any Form of Style becomes destructive of these ends, it is the Right of the Style Diva to alter or to abolish it, and to institute a new Style, laying its foundation on such Colors, Textures, and Shapes and organizing its Arrangements in such form that they shall seem most likely to effect her Happiness.

Look at how our culture views artists, writers, musicians, actors, directors. Why do we so admire those who create? It's not just because their product pleases us (although that's part of it).

185

Declaration of Creative Independence

We hold these truths to be self-evident: that all Style Divas are created equal, that they are endowed by their Creator with certain inalienable Rights: that among these are Life, Liberty, and the pursuit of Happiness...

Whenever any Form of Style becomes destructive of these ends, it is the Right of the Style Diva to alter or abolish it, and institute a new Style, laying its foundation on such Colors, Textures, and Shapes and organizing its Arrangements in such form that shall seem most likely to effect her Happiness.

Much of our admiration comes from how they embody freedom and risk-taking. They see "something" in what others call "nothing" and make it happen.

It's the same with people who build companies. **Driven by their sense of freedom and willingness to express themselves no matter what others think, these visionaries set the tone of things for the world at large—whether they are artists or business people—or both! They make a mark, build a legacy. That is Style.**

Diva
D R I L L : Write Your Declaration of Creative Independence

Now you're going to declare your own independence. What conventions, fears, and restrictions are holding you back when you're trying to create? Have you let yourself get locked into one style and can't seem to break free? Whom have you crowned queen, when you should be electing your own Style Diva as the chief of state? Consider all of these, then write them off—literally!—in your Declaration of Creative Independence.

POP QUIZ

Have you reached the heights of your creativity? Test your advanced Style Diva know-how and never stop that swagger.

1 **True or false: You should settle for nothing less than perfection.**

2 **If you don't like the way something has turned out and you want to scrap it right away, how long should you wait before making that decision?**

3 **What is a Style Diva's take on trends?**

4 **When you're stuck in a rut making choices, what's a good trick to use?**

5 **Name an important concept to remember when combining different styles.**

6 **If a project isn't going well, should you move on and forget about it?**

7 **What's the most creative time of the day (or night) for you to get styling?**

8 **Describe one of the secret ingredients of success in all creative endeavors.**

9 **Name three of your own signature style rules.**

10 **What is the Circle of Style, and how can you apply it to your Diva-full life?**

Style Divas
don't like
'the end'—
they prefer
'to be continued...'

Acknowledgments

This book would never have happened without the help of an entire team of people, starting with my publisher, David Dunham. David, you are a true visionary, and I cannot thank you enough for understanding my vision and letting me create this book freely. I am forever grateful for all of your support and help in pursuing my goals.

Huge thank-yous to Cindy Games and Ramona Wilkes for the long days, late nights, and early morning e-mails back and forth to get *Style Diva* done.

And giant kudos to the sales and marketing team of Laura, Brian, Paul, Sonya, Mark, Doug M., Charlie, Sally, Rick, Heather, Doug C., Susan, Anita, Dave, Trish, Dan, Kathleen, Lisa, Scott, and everyone else for your part in getting *Style Diva* into the hands of the most important people: the readers.

And I can't say enough about my stellar associates and staff, Ryan London and Thurayya Hernandez. Thank you both for getting on the *Style Diva* bandwagon, for having so much fun creating this book with me, for encouraging me every day, and for helping me achieve my goals in all areas. I depend on you so much, and you always come through for me. You are the ultimate cheerleaders and friends—and true Style Divas! I love you both.

And my dear Eva, thank you for making sure my little chicklins, Hutton and Hailey, were always fed and taken care of while I was working around the clock on so many deadlines.

Thank you, Brian Tofolli, my styling buddy, for always being there to dive in and help me with anything and everything I needed. You are so loving and so talented.

To Jonathan Small and Stacia Jesner, thanks for jumping in to help me with my manuscript. Your creative input and wonderful spirit during crunch time never went unnoticed.

And to the Anderson Thomas Design team: You hit the Style Diva groove and there was no stopping you. Thank you for understanding my creative vision and process. It was so much fun creating with your talented team. You guys are amazing!

Thank you to my many, many partners: Mervyns, Magid Gloves, Calyx & Corolla, QVC, and all of the others. You are true partners, and I appreciate how supportive you have all been of me and my endeavors. I feel so lucky to be able to work with you and your incredible teams. I love creating with you every day!

A big thank you to my literary agents, Jan Miller and Michael Broussard, who have helped me make my dream of being an author a reality, over and over again.

And last (but certainly not least), to Michael Stone, Allison Ames, Paula Friedman, and Jodi Rothman of The Beanstalk Group who help me every day to build my empire of style in all areas, whether in licensing, television, or publishing. I can't believe I get to work with such talent, and it is an incredible honor to be part of your group.

The fun and exhilaration I feel working with all of you is beyond description, and I feel so lucky that I get to play and create with all of you every day. This is my dream come true, and from the bottom of my heart, I thank all of you for being part of my dreams and my life!

Susie

About the Author

Susie Coelho is the consummate Style Diva and is a leading expert and trusted authority in the lifestyle industry. With years of experience in home, garden, and entertaining she inspires others to create beauty in their everyday lives.

As a best-selling author, celebrity spokesperson, television host, and product designer, her image and voice speak to an emerging desire for individuality. Susie's signature global style comes from her unique background. Born in England of East Indian/Portuguese heritage, she was brought up in Paris and Washington, DC. Always a world traveler, she brings an eclectic eye to style, trends, color, and design.

Her career started as a Ford model in New York City. From there, she quickly took her poise and confidence to the television screen as an actress and television host. As one of the forerunners in the makeover genre, *Surprise Gardener* launched her ten-year run on Home and Garden Television (HGTV). It was soon followed by her show, *Outer Spaces*.

Susie is the designer of Susie Coelho Style™, a collection of bedding, bath, tabletop, and home décor exclusively for Mervyns. She has also developed the Susie Coelho Outdoor™ collection of garden gloves and accessories with innovative style, function, and fit. With Calyx & Corolla, a luxury bouquet company, Susie lends her expert eye to create an exciting new series of floral arrangements. She will also be bringing her signature style to QVC.

To follow her two best-selling books, *Everyday Styling* and *Styling for Entertaining*, Coelho is launching a five-book series on style, starting with *Secrets of a Style Diva*, followed by *Style Your Dream Wedding*. Always pushing the envelope, Susie goes beyond the conventional to give her readers a fresh, exciting, and personal take on finding themselves in the process of styling their world.

In her Los Angeles home, Susie finds her own inspiration from her two young children Hutton and Hailey Dior.

For more about Susie Coelho or her collections visit her website at www.susiecoelho.com.